TRADING

IN THE

ZONE

TRADING IN THE ZONE

MASTER THE MARKET WITH CONFIDENCE, DISCIPLINE AND A WINNING ATTITUDE

MARK DOUGLAS

Foreword by Thom Hartle

NEW YORK INSTITUTE OF FINANCE

NEW YORK • TORONTO • SYDNEY • TOKYO • SINGAPORE

NEW YORK INSTITUTE OF FINANCE
An Imprint of Prentice Hall Press
A member of Penguin Putnam Inc.
375 Hudson Street, New York, N.Y. 10014
www.penguinputnam.com

LIBRARY OF CONGRESS CATALOGING-IN-PUBLICATION DATA

Douglas, Mark (Mark J.)
Trading in the zone : master the market with confidence, discipline, and a winning
attitude / by Mark Douglas.
p.   cm.
ISBN 0-7352-0144-7 (cloth)
1. Stocks.   2. Speculation.   I. Title.

HG6041.D59 2001
332.64—dc21   00   045251

Printed in the United States of America

18 19 20

This publication is designed to provide accurate and authoritative information in regard
to the subject matter covered. It is sold with the understanding that the publisher is not
engaged in rendering legal, accounting, or other professional service. If legal advice or
other expert assistance is required, the services of a competent professional person
should be sought.

*. . . From the Declaration of Principles jointly adopted by a Committee of the American
Bar Association and a Committee of Publishers and Associations.*

Most Prentice Hall Press Books are available at special quantity discounts for
bulk purchases for sales promotions, premiums, fund-raising, or educational use.
Special books, or book excerpts, can also be created to fit specific needs.

For details, write: Special Markets, Penguin Putnam Inc., 375 Hudson Street,
New York, New York 10014.

NYIF and NEW YORK INSTITUTE OF FINANCE are trademarks of Executive Tax
Reports, Inc. used under license by Prentice Hall Direct, Inc.

DEDICATION

This book is dedicated to all of the traders I have had the pleasure of working with over the last 18 years as a trading coach. Each of you in your own unique way is a part of the insight and guidance this book will provide to those who choose to trade from a confident, disciplined, and consistent state of mind.

TABLE OF CONTENTS

CHAPTER 1

THE ROAD TO SUCCESS: FUNDAMENTAL, TECHNICAL, OR MENTAL ANALYSIS?

CHAPTER 2

THE LURE (AND THE DANGERS) OF TRADING

CHAPTER 11

THINKING LIKE A TRADER

FOREWORD

The great bull market in stocks has led to an equally great bull market in the number of books published on the subject of how to make money *trading* the markets. Many ideas abound, some good, some not, some original, some just a repackaging of earlier works. Occasionally, though, a writer comes forward with something that really sets him or her apart from the pack, something special. One such writer is Mark Douglas.

Mark Douglas, in *Trading in the Zone*, has written a book that is the accumulation of years of thought and research—the work of a lifetime—and for those of us who view trading as a profession, he has produced a gem.

Trading in the Zone is an in-depth look at the challenges that we face when we take up the challenge of trading. To the novice, the only challenge appears to be to find a way to make money. Once the novice learns that tips, brokers' advice, and other ways to justify buying or selling do not work consistently, he discovers that he either needs to develop a reliable trading strategy or purchase one. After that, trading *should* be easy, right? All you have to do is follow the rules, and the money will fall into your lap.

At this point, if not before, novices discover that trading can turn into one of the most frustrating experiences they will ever face. This experience leads to the oft-started statistic that 95 percent of futures traders lose all of their money within the first year of trading. Stock traders generally experience the same results, which is why pundits always point to the fact that most stock traders fail to outperform a simple buy and hold investment scenario.

So, why do people, the majority of whom are extremely successful in other occupations, fail so miserably as traders? Are successful traders born and not made? Mark Douglas says no. What's necessary, he says, is that the individual acquire the trader's mindset.

It sounds easy, but the fact is, this mindset is very foreign when compared with the way our life experiences teach us to think about the world.

That 95-percent failure rate makes sense when you consider how most of us experience life, using skills learned as we grow. When it comes to trading, however, it turns out that the skills we learn to earn high marks in school, advance our careers, and create relationships with other people, the skills we are taught that should carry us through life, turn out to be inappropriate for trading. Traders, we find out, must learn to think in terms of probabilities and to surrender all of the skills we have acquired to achieve in virtually every other aspect of our lives. In *Trading in the Zone*, Mark Douglas teaches us how. He has put together a very valuable book. His sources are his own personal experiences as a trader, a trader's coach in Chicago, author, and lecturer in his field of trading psychology.

My recommendation? Enjoy Douglas's *Trading in the Zone* and, in doing so, develop a trader's mindset.

THOM HARTLE

PREFACE

The goal of any trader is to turn profits on a regular basis, yet so few people ever really make consistent money as traders. What accounts for the small percentage of traders who are consistently successful? To me, the determining factor is psychological—the consistent winners think differently from everyone else.

I started trading in 1978. At the time, I was managing a commercial casualty insurance agency in the suburbs of Detroit, Michigan. I had a very successful career and thought I could easily transfer that success into trading. Unfortunately, I found that was not the case. By 1981, I was thoroughly disgusted with my inability to trade effectively while holding another job, so I moved to Chicago and got a job as a broker with Merrill Lynch at the Chicago Board of Trade. How did I do? Well, within nine months of moving to Chicago, I had lost nearly everything I owned. My losses were the result of both my trading activities and my exorbitant life style, which demanded that I make a lot of money as a trader.

From these early experiences as a trader, I learned an enormous amount about myself, and about the role of psychology in trading. As a result, in 1982, I started working on my first book, *The Disciplined Trader: Developing Winning Attitudes*. When I began this project I had no concept of how difficult it was to write a book or explain something that I understood for myself in a manner and form that would be useful to other people. I thought it was going to take me between six and nine months to get the job done. It took seven and a half years and was finally published by Prentice Hall in 1990.

In 1983, I left Merrill Lynch to start a consulting firm, Trading Behavior Dynamics, where I presently develop and conduct seminars on trading psychology and act in the capacity of what is commonly referred to as a trading coach. I've done countless presentations for trading companies, clearing firms, brokerage houses, banks, and investment conferences all over the world. I've worked at a personal level, one on one, with virtually every type of trader in the business, including some of the biggest floor traders, hedgers, option specialists, and CTAs, as well as neophytes

As of this writing, I have spent the last seventeen years dissecting the psychological dynamics behind trading so that I could develop effective methods for teaching the proper principles of success. What I've discovered is that, at the most fundamental level, there is a problem with the way we think. There is something inherent in the way our minds work that doesn't fit very well with the characteristics shown by the markets.

Those traders who have confidence in their own trades, who trust themselves to do what needs to be done without hesitation, are the ones who become successful. They no longer fear the erratic behavior of the market. They learn to focus on the information that helps them spot opportunities to make a profit, rather than focusing on the information that reinforces their fears.

While this may sound complicated, it all boils down to learning to believe that: (1) you don't need to know what's going to happen next to make money; (2) anything can happen; and (3) every moment is unique, meaning every edge and outcome is truly a unique experience. The trade either works or it doesn't. In any case, you wait for the next edge to appear and go through the process again and again. With this approach you will learn in a methodical, non-random fashion what works and what doesn't. And, just as important, you will build a sense of self-trust so that you won't damage yourself in an environment that has the unlimited qualities the markets have.

Most traders don't believe that their trading problems are the result of the way they think about trading or, more specifically, how they are thinking while they are trading. In my first book, *The Disciplined Trader*, I identified the problems confronting the trader from a mental perspective and then built a philosophical framework for understanding the nature of these problems and why they exist. I had five major objectives in mind in writing *Trading in the Zone*:

- To prove to the trader that more or better market analysis is not the solution to his trading difficulties or lack of consistent results.

- To convince the trader that it's his attitude and "state of mind" that determine his results.

- To provide the trader with the specific beliefs and attitudes that are necessary to build a winner's mindset, which means learning how to think in probabilities.

- To address the many conflicts, contradictions, and paradoxes in thinking that cause the typical trader to assume that he already does think in probabilities, when he really doesn't.

- To take the trader through a process that integrates this thinking strategy into his mental system at a functional level.

(*Note:* Until recently, most traders were men, but I recognize that more and more women are joining the ranks. In an effort to avoid confusion and awkward phrasing, I have consistently used the pronoun "he" throughout this book in describing traders. This certainly does not reflect any bias on my part.)

Trading in the Zone presents a serious psychological approach to becoming a consistent winner in your trading. I do not offer a trading system; I am more interested in showing you how to think in the way necessary to become a profitable trader. I assume that you already have your own system, your own edge. You must learn to trust your edge. The edge means there is a higher probability of one outcome than another. The greater your confidence, the easier it will be to execute your trades. This book is designed to give you the insight and understanding you need about yourself and the nature of trading, so that actually doing it becomes as easy, simple, and stress-free as when you're just watching the market and thinking about doing it.

In order to determine how well you "think like a trader," take the following Attitude Survey. There are no right or wrong answers.

Your answers are an indication of how consistent your current mental framework is with the way you need to think in order to get the most out of your trading.

MARK DOUGLAS

ATTITUDE SURVEY

1. To make money as a trader you have to know what the market is going to do next.

   Agree   **· Disagree**

2. Sometimes I find myself thinking that there must be a way to trade without having to take a loss.

   Agree   **·Disagree**

3. Making money as a trader is primarily a function of analysis.

   'Agree   **Disagree**

4. Losses are an unavoidable component of trading.

   · Agree   **Disagree**

5. My risk is always defined before I enter a trade.

   ·Agree   **Disagree**

6. In my mind there is always a cost associated with finding out what the market may do next.

   · Agree   **Disagree**

7. I wouldn't even bother putting on the next trade if I wasn't sure that it was going to be a winner.

   Agree   **· Disagree**

8. The more a trader learns about the markets and how they behave, the easier it will be for him to execute his trades.

   'Agree   **Disagree**

9. My methodology tells me exactly under what market conditions to either enter or exit a trade.

   `Agree   Disagree

10. Even when I have a clear signal to reverse my position, I find it extremely difficult to do.

   `Agree   Disagree

11. I have sustained periods of consistent success usually followed by some fairly drastic draw-downs in my equity.

   `Agree   Disagree

12. When I first started trading I would describe my trading methodology as haphazard, meaning some success in between a lot of pain.

   `Agree   Disagree

13. I often find myself feeling that the markets are against me personally.

   Agree   `Disagree

14. As much as I might try to "let go," I find it very difficult to put past emotional wounds behind me.

   `Agree   Disagree

15. I have a money management philosophy that is founded in the principle of always taking some money out of the market when the market makes it available.

   `Agree   Disagree

16. A trader's job is to identify patterns in the markets' behavior that represent an opportunity and then to determine the risk of find-

ing out if these patterns will play themselves out as they have in the past.

'Agree   **Disagree**

17. Sometimes I just can't help feeling that I am a victim of the market.

    Agree   **' Disagree**

18. When I trade I usually try to stay focused in one time frame.

    'Agree   **Disagree**

19. Trading successfully requires a degree of mental flexibility far beyond the scope of most people.

    Agree   **' Disagree**

20. There are times when I can definitely feel the flow of the market; however, I often have difficulty acting on these feelings.

    Agree   **' Disagree**

21. There are many times when I am in a profitable trade and I know the move is basically over, but I still won't take my profits.

    Agree   **'Disagree**

22. No matter how much money I make in a trade, I am rarely ever satisfied and feel that I could have made more.

    Agree   **' Disagree**

23. When I put on a trade, I feel I have a positive attitude. I anticipate all of the money I could make from the trade in a positive way.

    'Agree   **Disagree**

24. The most important component in a trader's ability to accumulate money over time is having a belief in his own consistency.

    ' Agree   Disagree

25. If you were granted a wish to be able to instantaneously acquire one trading skill, what skill would you choose?

    _____

26. I often spend sleepless nights worrying about the market.

    Agree   ' Disagree

27. Do you ever feel compelled to make a trade because you are afraid that you might miss out?

    Yes   ↝ No

28. Although it doesn't happen very often, I really like my trades to be perfect. When I make a perfect call it feels so good that it makes up for all of the times that I don't.

    Agree   ﹨ Disagree

29. Do you ever find yourself planning trades you never execute, and executing trades you never planned?

    Yes   ' No

30. In a few sentences explain why most traders either don't make money or aren't able to keep what they make.

    _____

    _____

    _____

    _____

Set aside your answers as you read through this book. After you've finished the last chapter ("Thinking Like a Trader"), take the Attitude Survey again—it's reprinted at the back of the book. You may be surprised to see how much your answers differ from the first time.

ACKNOWLEDGMENTS

I would especially like to thank all of the traders who bought the signed limited edition manuscript of the first seven chapters of this book. Your feedback gave me the inspiration to add the additional four chapters.

Next, I would like to thank fellow traders Robert St. John, Greg Bieber, Joe Cowell, Larry Pesavento, and Ted Hearne for their friendship and the special ways in which each of them contributed to the development of this book.

I would also like to acknowledge my friend, Eileen Bruno, for editing the original manuscript; and, at Prentice Hall, Ellen Schneid Coleman, Associate Publisher, for her professionalism and help in smoothing the path to publication, and Barry Richardson, Development Editor, for his help in shaping the preface, and Thomas Hartle, for graciously writing the foreword. Their time and talent are greatly appreciated.

CHAPTER 1

THE ROAD TO SUCCESS:
FUNDAMENTAL, TECHNICAL, OR MENTAL ANALYSIS?

IN THE BEGINNING: FUNDAMENTAL ANALYSIS

Who remembers when fundamental analysis was considered the only real or proper way to make trading decisions? When I started trading in 1978, technical analysis was used by only a handful of traders, who were considered by the rest of the market community to be, at the very least, crazy. As difficult as it is to believe now, it wasn't very long ago when Wall Street and most of the major funds and financial institutions thought that technical analysis was some form of mystical hocus-pocus.

Now, of course, just the opposite is true. Almost all experienced traders use some form of technical analysis to help them formulate their trading strategies. Except for some small, isolated pockets in the academic community, the "purely" fundamental analyst is virtually extinct. What caused this dramatic shift in perspective?

I'm sure it's no surprise to anyone that the answer to this question is very simple: Money! The problem with making trading decisions from a strictly fundamental perspective is the inherent difficulty of making money consistently using this approach.

For those of you who may not be familiar with fundamental analysis, let me explain. Fundamental analysis attempts to take into consideration all the variables that could affect the relative balance or imbalance between the supply of and the possible demand for any particular stock, commodity, or financial instrument. Using primarily mathematical models that weigh the significance of a variety of factors (interest rates, balance sheets, weather patterns, and numerous others), the analyst projects what the price should be at some point in the future.

The problem with these models is that they rarely, if ever, factor in other traders as variables. People, expressing their beliefs and expectations about the future, make prices move—not models. The fact that a model makes a logical and reasonable projection based on all the relevant variables is not of much value if the traders who are responsible for most of the trading volume are not aware of the model or don't believe in it.

As a matter of fact, many traders, especially those on the floors of the futures exchanges who have the ability to move prices very dramatically in one direction or the other, usually don't have the slightest concept of the fundamental supply and demand factors that are supposed to affect prices. Furthermore, at any given moment, much of their trading activity is prompted by a response to emotional factors that are completely outside the parameters of the fundamental model. In other words, the people who trade (and consequently move prices) don't always act in a rational manner.

Ultimately, the fundamental analyst could find that a prediction about where prices should be at some point in the future is correct. But in the meantime, price movement could be so volatile that it would be very difficult, if not impossible, to stay in a trade in order to realize the objective.

THE SHIFT TO TECHNICAL ANALYSIS

Technical analysis has been around for as long as there have been organized markets in the form of exchanges. But the trading community didn't accept technical analysis as a viable tool for making money until the late 1970s or early 1980s. Here's what the technical analyst knew that it took the mainstream market community generations to catch on to.

A finite number of traders participate in the markets on any given day, week, or month. Many of these traders do the same kinds of things over and over in their attempt to make money. In other words, individuals develop behavior patterns, and a group of individuals, interacting with one another on a consistent basis, form collective behavior patterns. These behavior patterns are observable and quantifiable, and they repeat themselves with statistical reliability.

Technical analysis is a method that organizes this collective behavior into identifiable patterns that can give a clear indication of when there is a greater probability of one thing happening over another. In a sense, technical analysis allows you to get into the mind of the market to anticipate what's likely to happen next, based on the kind of patterns the market generated at some previous moment.

As a method for projecting future price movement, technical analysis has turned out to be far superior to a purely fundamental approach. It keeps the trader focused on what the market is doing *now* in relation to what it has done in the past, instead of focusing on what the market should be doing based solely on what is logical and reasonable as determined by a mathematical model. On the other hand, fundamental analysis creates what I call a "reality gap" between "what should be" and "what is." The reality gap makes it extremely difficult to make anything but very long-term predictions that can be difficult to exploit, even if they are correct.

In contrast, technical analysis not only closes this reality gap, but also makes available to the trader a virtually unlimited number of possibilities to take advantage of. The technical approach opens up many more possibilities because it identifies how the same repeatable behavior patterns occur in every time frame—moment-to-moment, daily, weekly, yearly, and every time span in between. In other words, technical analysis turns the market into an endless stream of opportunities to enrich oneself.

THE SHIFT TO MENTAL ANALYSIS

If technical analysis works so well, why would more and more of the trading community shift their focus from technical analysis of the market to mental analysis of themselves, meaning their own individual trading psychology? To answer this question, you probably don't have to do anything more than ask yourself why you bought this book. The most likely reason is that you're dissatisfied with the difference between what you perceive as the unlimited potential to make money and what you end up with on the bottom line.

That's the problem with technical analysis, if you want to call it a problem. Once you learn to identify patterns and read the market, you find there are limitless opportunities to make money. But, as I'm sure you already know, there can also be a huge gap between what you understand about the markets, and your ability to transform that knowledge into consistent profits or a steadily rising equity curve.

Think about the number of times you've looked at a price chart and said to yourself, "Hmmm, it looks like the market is going up (or down, as the case may be)," and what you thought was going to happen actually happened. But you did nothing except watch the market move while you anguished over all the money you could have made.

There's a big difference between predicting that something will happen in the market (and thinking about all the money you could have made) and the reality of actually getting into and out of trades. I call this difference, and others like it, a "psychological gap" that can make trading one of the most difficult endeavors you could choose to undertake and certainly one of the most mysterious to master.

The big question is: Can trading be mastered? Is it possible to experience trading with the same ease and simplicity implied when you are only watching the market and thinking about success, as opposed to actually having to put on and take off trades? Not only is the answer an unequivocal "yes," but that's also exactly what this book is designed to give you—the insight and understanding you need about yourself and about the nature of trading. So the result is that actually doing it becomes as easy, simple, and stress-free as when you are just watching the market and thinking about doing it.

This may seem like a tall order, and to some of you it may even seem impossible. But it's not. There are people who have mastered the art of trading, who have closed the gap between the possibilities available and their bottom-line performance. But as you might expect, these winners are relatively few in number compared with the number of traders who experience varying degrees of frustration, all the way to extreme exasperation, wondering why they can't create the consistent success they so desperately desire.

In fact, the differences between these two groups of traders (the consistent winners and everyone else) are analogous to the differences between the Earth and the moon. The Earth and moon are both celestial bodies that exist in the same solar system, so they do have something in common. But they are as different in nature and characteristics as night and day. By the same token, anyone who puts on a trade can claim to be a trader, but when you compare the characteristics of the handful of consistent winners with the characteristics of most other traders, you'll find they're also as different as night and day.

If going to the moon represents consistent success as a trader, we can say that getting to the moon is possible. The journey is extremely difficult and only a handful of people have made it. From our perspective here on Earth, the moon is usually visible every night and it seems so close that we could just reach out and touch it. Trading successfully feels the same way. On any given day, week, or month, the markets make available vast amounts of money to anyone who has the capacity to put on a trade. Since the markets are in constant motion, this money is also constantly flowing, which makes the possibilities for success greatly magnified and seemingly within your grasp.

I use the word "seemingly" to make an important distinction between the two groups of traders. For those who have learned how to be consistent, or have broken through what I call the "threshold of consistency," the money is not only within their grasp; they can virtually take it at will. I'm sure that some will find this statement shocking or difficult to believe, but it is true. There are some limitations, but for the most part, money flows into the accounts of these traders with such ease and effortlessness that it literally boggles most people's minds.

However, for the traders who have not evolved into this select group, the word "seemingly" means exactly what it implies. It seems as if the consistency or ultimate success they desire is "at hand," or "within their grasp," just before it slips away or evaporates before their eyes, time and time again. The only thing about trading that is consistent with this group is emotional pain. Yes, they certainly have moments of elation, but it is not an exaggeration to say that most of the time they are in a state of fear, anger, frustration, anxiety, disappointment, betrayal, and regret.

So what separates these two groups of traders? Is it intelligence? Are the consistent winners just plain smarter than everyone else? Do they work harder? Are they better analysts, or do they have access to better trading systems? Do they possess inherent personality characteristics that make it easier for them to deal with the intense pressures of trading?

All of these possibilities sound quite plausible, except when you consider that most of the trading industry's failures are also some of society's brightest and most accomplished people. The largest group of consistent losers is composed primarily of doctors, lawyers, engineers, scientists, CEOs, wealthy retirees, and entrepreneurs. Furthermore, most of the industry's best market analysts are the worst traders imaginable. Intelligence and good market analysis can certainly contribute to success, but they are not the defining factors that separate the consistent winners from everyone else.

Well, if it isn't intelligence or better analysis, then what could it be?

Having worked with some of the best and some of the worst traders in the business, and having helped some of the worst become some of the best, I can state without a doubt that there are specific reasons why the best traders consistently out-perform everyone else. If I had to distill all of the reasons down to one, I would simply say that the best traders think differently from the rest.

I know that doesn't sound very profound, but it does have profound implications if you consider what it means to think differently. To one degree or another, all of us think differently from everyone else. We may not always be mindful of this fact, it seems natural to assume that other people share our perceptions and interpretations of events. In fact, this assumption continues to seem valid until we find ourselves in a basic, fundamental disagreement with someone about something we both experienced. Other than our physical features, the way we think is what makes us unique, probably even more unique than our physical features do.

Let's get back to traders. What is different about the way the best traders think as opposed to how those who are still struggling think? While the markets can be described as an arena of endless opportunities, they simultaneously confront the individual with some of the most sustained, adverse psychological conditions you can expose yourself to. At some point, everyone who trades learns something about the markets that will indicate when opportunities exist. But learning how to identify an opportunity to buy or sell does not mean that you have learned to think like a trader.

The defining characteristic that separates the consistent winners from everyone else is this: The winners have attained a mind-set—a unique set of attitudes—that allows them to remain disciplined, focused, and, above all, confident in spite of the adverse conditions. As a result, they are no longer susceptible to the common fears and trading errors that plague everyone else. Everyone who trades ends up learning something about the markets; very few people who trade ever learn the attitudes that are absolutely essential to becoming a consistent winner. Just as people can learn to perfect the proper technique for swinging a golf club or tennis racket, their consistency, or lack of it, will without a doubt come from their attitude

Traders who make it beyond "the threshold of consistency" usually experience a great deal of pain (both emotional and financial) before they acquire the kind of attitude that allows them to function effectively in the market environment. The rare exceptions are usually those who were born into successful trading families or who started their trading careers under the guidance of someone who understood the true nature of trading, and, just as important, knew how to teach it.

Why are emotional pain and financial disaster common among traders? The simple answer is that most of us weren't fortunate enough to start our trading careers with the proper guidance. However, the reasons go much deeper than this. I have spent the last seventeen years dissecting the psychological dynamics behind trading so that I could develop effective methods for teaching the principles of success. What I've discovered is that trading is chock full of paradoxes and contradictions in thinking that make it extremely difficult to learn how to be successful. In fact, if I had to choose one word that encapsulates the nature of trading, it would be "paradox." (According to the dictionary, a paradox is something that seems to have contradictory qualities or that is contrary to common belief or what generally makes sense to people.)

Financial and emotional disaster are common among traders because many of the perspectives, attitudes, and principles that would otherwise make perfect sense and work quite well in our daily lives have the opposite effect in the trading environment. They just don't work. Not knowing this, most traders start their careers with a fundamental lack of understanding of what it means to be a trader, the skills that are involved, and the depth to which those skills need to be developed.

Here is a prime example of what I am talking about: Trading is inherently risky. To my knowledge, no trade has a guaranteed outcome; therefore, the possibility of being wrong and losing money is always present. So when you put on a trade, can you consider yourself a risk-taker? Even though this may sound like a trick question, it is not.

The logical answer to the question is, unequivocally, yes. If I engage in an activity that is inherently risky, then I must be a risk-taker. This is a perfectly reasonable assumption for any trader to make. In fact, not only do virtually all traders make this assumption, but most traders take pride in thinking of themselves as risk-takers.

The problem is that this assumption couldn't be further from the truth. Of course, any trader is taking a risk when you put on a trade, but that doesn't mean that you are correspondingly accepting that risk. In other words, all trades are risky because the outcomes are probable—not guaranteed. But do most traders really believe they are taking a risk when they put on a trade? Have they really accepted that the trade has a non-guaranteed, probable outcome? Furthermore, have they fully accepted the possible consequences?

The answer is, unequivocally, no! Most traders have absolutely no concept of what it means to be a risk-taker in the way a successful trader thinks about risk. The best traders not only take the risk, they have also learned to accept and embrace that risk. There is a huge psychological gap between assuming you are a risk taker because you put on trades and fully accepting the risks inherent in each trade. When you fully accept the risks, it will have profound implications on your bottom-line performance.

The best traders can put on a trade without the slightest bit of hesitation or conflict, and just as freely and without hesitation or conflict, admit it isn't working. They can get out of the trade—even with a loss—and doing so doesn't resonate the slightest bit of emotional discomfort. In other words, the risks inherent in trading do not cause the best traders to lose their discipline, focus, or sense of confidence. If you are unable to trade without the slightest bit of emotional discomfort (specifically, fear), then you have not learned how to accept the risks inherent in trading. This is a big problem, because to whatever degree you haven't accepted the risk, is the same degree to which you will avoid the risk. Trying to avoid something that is unavoidable will have disastrous effects on your ability to trade successfully.

Learning to truly accept the risks in any endeavor can be difficult, but it is extremely difficult for traders, especially considering what's at stake. What are we generally most afraid of (besides dying or public speaking)? Certainly, losing money and being wrong both rank close to the top of the list. Admitting we are wrong and losing money to boot can be extremely painful, and certainly something to avoid. Yet as traders, we are confronted with these two possibilities virtually every moment we are in a trade.

Now, you might be saying to yourself, "Apart from the fact that it hurts so much, it's natural to not want to be wrong and lose something; therefore, it's appropriate for me to do whatever I can to avoid it." I agree with you. But it is also this natural tendency that makes trading (which looks like it should be easy) extremely difficult.

Trading presents us with a fundamental paradox: How do we remain disciplined, focused, and confident in the face of constant uncertainty? When you have learned how to "think" like a trader, that's exactly what you'll be able to do. Learning how to redefine your trading activities in a way that allows you to completely accept the risk is the key to thinking like a successful trader. Learning to accept the risk is a trading skill—the most important skill you can learn. Yet it's rare that developing traders focus any attention or expend any effort to learn it.

When you learn the trading skill of risk acceptance, the market will not be able to generate information that you define or interpret as painful. If the information the market generates doesn't have the potential to cause you emotional pain, there's nothing to avoid. It is just information, telling you what the possibilities are. This is called an objective perspective—one that is not skewed or distorted by what you are afraid is going to happen or not happen.

I'm sure there isn't one trader reading this book who hasn't gotten into trades too soon—before the market has actually generated a signal, or too late—long after the market has generated a signal. What trader hasn't convinced himself not to take a loss and, as a result, had it turn into a bigger one; or got out of winning trades too soon; or found himself in winning trades but didn't take any profits at all, and then let the trades turn into losers; or moved stop-losses closer to his entry point, only to get stopped out and have the market go back in his direction? These are but a few of the many errors traders perpetuate upon themselves time and time again.

These are not market-generated errors. That is, these errors do not come from the market. The market is neutral, in the sense that it moves and generates information about itself. Movement and information provide each of us with the opportunity to do something, but that's all! The markets don't have any power over the unique way in which each of us perceives and interprets this information, or control of the decisions and actions we take as a result. The errors I already mentioned and many more are strictly the result of what I call "faulty trading attitudes and perspectives." Faulty attitudes that foster fear instead of trust and confidence.

I don't think I could put the difference between the consistent winners and everyone else more simply than this: The best traders aren't afraid. They aren't afraid because they have developed attitudes that give them the greatest degree of mental flexibility to flow in and out of trades based on what the market is telling them about the possibilities from its perspective. At the same time, the best traders have developed attitudes that prevent them from getting reckless. Everyone else is afraid, to some degree or another. When they're not afraid, they have the tendency to become reckless and to create the kind of experience for themselves that will cause them to be afraid from that point on.

Ninety-five percent of the trading errors you are likely to make—causing the money to just evaporate before your eyes—will stem from your attitudes about being wrong, losing money, missing out, and leaving money on the table. What I call the four primary trading fears.

Now, you may be saying to yourself, "I don't know about this: I've always thought traders should have a healthy fear of the markets." Again, this is a perfectly logical and reasonable assumption. But when it comes to trading, your fears will act against you in such a way that you will cause the very thing you are afraid of to actually happen. If you're afraid of being wrong, your fear will act upon your perception of market information in a way that will cause you to do something that ends up making you wrong.

When you are fearful, no other possibilities exist. You can't perceive other possibilities or act on them properly, even if you did manage to perceive them, because fear is immobilizing. Physically, it causes us to freeze or run. Mentally, it causes us to narrow our focus of attention to the object of our fear. This means that thoughts about other possibilities, as well as other available information from the market, get blocked. You won't think about all the rational things you've learned about the market until you are no longer afraid and the event is over. Then you will think to yourself, "I knew that. Why didn't I think of it then?" or, "Why couldn't I act on it then?"

It's extremely difficult to perceive that the source of these problems is our own inappropriate attitudes. That's what makes fear so insidious. Many of the thinking patterns that adversely affect our trading are a function of the natural ways in which we were brought up to think and see the world. These thinking patterns are so deeply ingrained that it rarely occurs to us that the source of our trading difficulties is internal, derived from our state of mind. Indeed, it seems much more natural to see the source of a problem as external, in the market, because it feels like the market is causing our pain, frustration, and dissatisfaction.

Obviously these are abstract concepts and certainly not something most traders are going to concern themselves with. Yet understanding the relationship between beliefs, attitudes, and perception is as fundamental to trading as learning how to serve is to tennis, or as learning how to swing a club is to golf. Put another way, understanding and controlling your perception of market information is important only to the extent that you want to achieve consistent results.

I say this because there is something else about trading that is as true as the statement I just made: You don't have to know anything about yourself or the markets to put on a winning trade, just as you don't have to know the proper way to swing a tennis racket or golf club in order to hit a good shot from time to time. The first time I played golf, I hit several good shots throughout the game even though I hadn't learned any particular technique; but my score was still over 120 for 18 holes. Obviously, to improve my overall score, I needed to learn technique.

Of course, the same is true for trading. We need technique to achieve consistency. But what technique? This is truly one of the most perplexing aspects of learning how to trade effectively. If we aren't aware of, or don't understand, how our beliefs and attitudes affect our perception of market information, it will seem as if it is the market's behavior that is causing the lack of consistency. As a result, it would stand to reason that the best way to avoid losses and become consistent would be to learn more about the markets.

This bit of logic is a trap that almost all traders fall into at some point, and it seems to make perfect sense. But this approach doesn't work. The market simply offers too many—often conflicting—variables to consider. Furthermore, there are no limits to the market's behavior. It can do anything at any moment. As a matter of fact, because every person who trades is a market variable, it can be said that any single trader can cause virtually anything to happen.

This means that no matter how much you learn about the market's behavior, no matter how brilliant an analyst you become, you will never learn enough to anticipate every possible way that the market can make you wrong or cause you to lose money. So if you are afraid of being wrong or losing money, it means you will never learn enough to compensate for the negative effects these fears will have on your ability to be objective and your ability to act without hesitation. In other words, you won't be confident in the face of constant uncertainty. The hard, cold reality of trading is that every trade has an uncertain outcome. Unless you learn to completely accept the possibility of an uncertain outcome, you will try either consciously or unconsciously to avoid any possibility you define as painful. In the process, you will subject yourself to any number of self-generated, costly errors.

Now, I am not suggesting that we don't need some form of market analysis or methodology to define opportunities and allow us to recognize them; we certainly do. However, market analysis is not the path to consistent results. It will not solve the trading problems created by lack of confidence, lack of discipline, or improper focus.

When you operate from the assumption that more or better analysis will create consistency, you will be driven to gather as many market variables as possible into your arsenal of trading tools. But what happens then? You are still disappointed and betrayed by the markets, time and again, because of something you didn't see or give enough consideration to. It will feel like you can't trust the markets; but the reality is, you can't trust yourself.

Confidence and fear are contradictory states of mind that both stem from our beliefs and attitudes. To be confident, functioning in an environment where you can easily lose more than you intend to risk, requires absolute trust in yourself. However, you won't be able to achieve that trust until you have trained your mind to override your natural inclination to think in ways that are counterproductive to being a consistently successful trader. Learning how to analyze the market's behavior is simply not the appropriate training.

You have two choices: You can try to eliminate risk by learning about as many market variables as possible. (I call this the black hole of analysis, because it is the path of ultimate frustration.) Or you can learn how to redefine your trading activities in such a way that you truly accept the risk, and you're no longer afraid.

When you've achieved a state of mind where you truly accept the risk, you won't have the potential to define and interpret market information in painful ways. When you eliminate the potential to define market information in painful ways, you also eliminate the tendency to rationalize, hesitate, jump the gun, hope that the market will give you money, or hope that the market will save you from your inability to cut your losses.

As long as you are susceptible to the kinds of errors that are the result of rationalizing, justifying, hesitating, hoping, and jumping the gun, you will not be able to trust yourself. If you can't trust yourself to be objective and to always act in your own best interests, achieving consistent results will be next to impossible. Trying to do something that looks so simple may well be the most exasperating thing you will ever attempt to do. The irony is that, when you have the appropriate attitude, when you have acquired a "trader's mind-set" and can remain confident in the face of constant uncertainty, trading will be as easy and simple as you probably thought it was when you first started out.

So, what is the solution? You will need to learn how to adjust your attitudes and beliefs about trading in such a way that you can trade without the slightest bit of fear, but at the same time keep a framework in place that does not allow you to become reckless. That's exactly what this book is designed to teach you.

As you move ahead, I would like you to keep something in mind. The successful trader that you want to become is a future projection of yourself that you have to grow into. Growth implies expansion, learning, and creating a new way of expressing yourself. This is true even if you're already a successful trader and are reading this book to become more successful. Many of the new ways in which you will learn to express yourself will be in direct conflict with ideas and beliefs you presently hold about the nature of trading. You may or may not already be aware of some of these beliefs. In any case, what you currently hold to be true about the nature of trading will argue to keep things just the way they are, in spite of your frustrations and unsatisfying results.

These internal arguments are natural. My challenge in this book is to help you resolve these arguments as efficiently as possible. Your willingness to consider that other possibilities exist—possibilities that you may not be aware of or may not have given enough consideration to—will obviously make the learning process faster and easier.

CHAPTER 2

THE LURE
(AND THE DANGERS)
OF TRADING

In January 1994, I was asked to speak at a trading conference in Chicago, sponsored by *Futures Magazine*. At one of the luncheons I happened to be sitting next to an editor for one of the major publishers of books about trading. We were having a lively conversation about why so few people become successful at trading, even people who are otherwise very accomplished. At one point, the editor asked me if a possible explanation for this phenomenon might be that people were getting into trading for the wrong reasons.

THE ATTRACTION

I had to pause for a moment to think about this. I agree that many of the typical reasons people are motivated to trade—the action, euphoria, desire to be a hero, the attention one can draw to himself by winning, or the self-pity that comes from losing—create problems that will ultimately detract from a trader's performance and overall success. But the true underlying attraction to trading is far more fundamental and universal. Trading is an activity that offers the individual

17

unlimited freedom of creative expression, a freedom of expression that has been denied most of us for most of our lives.

Of course, the editor asked me what I meant by this. I explained that in the trading environment, we make almost all of the rules. This means there are very few restrictions or boundaries on how we can choose to express ourselves. Of course there are some formalities such as having to become a member of an exchange to be a floor trader, or meeting the minimum financial requirements to open a brokerage account if you're an off-the-floor trader. But otherwise, once you are in a position to start trading, the possibilities that exist for how you go about doing it are virtually limitless.

I went on to give him an example from a seminar I attended several years ago. Someone had calculated that, if you combined bond futures, bond options, and the cash bond markets, there would be over eight billion possible spread combinations. Now add the timing considerations based on how you read the prevailing market conditions, and the various ways to trade become virtually limitless.

The editor paused for a moment and asked, "But why would having access to such an unrestricted environment result in fairly consistent failure?" I answered, "Because unlimited possibilities coupled with the unlimited freedom to take advantage of those possibilities present the individual with unique and specialized psychological challenges, challenges that very few people are properly equipped to deal with, or have any awareness of for that matter, and people can't exactly work on overcoming something if they don't even know it's a problem."

The freedom is great. All of us seem to naturally want it, strive for it, even crave it. But that doesn't mean that we have the appropriate psychological resources to operate effectively in an environment that has few, if any, boundaries and where the potential to do enormous damage to ourselves exists. Almost everyone needs to make some mental adjustments, regardless of their educational background, intelligence or how successful they've been in other endeavors.

The kind of adjustments I'm talking about have to do with cre-ating an internal mental structure that provides the trader with the greatest degree of balance between the freedom to do anything and the potential that exists to experience both the financial and psychological damage that can be a direct result of that freedom.

Creating a mental structure can be difficult enough, especially if what you want to instill is in conflict with what you already believe. But for those of us who want to be traders, the difficulty of creating the appropriate structure is invariably compounded by a backlog of mental resistance that starts developing at the very earliest stages of our lives.

All of us are born into some sort of social environment. A social environment (or society), whether it's a family, city, state, or country, implies the existence of structure. Social structures consist of rules, restrictions, boundaries, and a set of beliefs that become a code of behavior that limits the ways in which individuals within that social structure can or cannot express themselves. Furthermore, most of the limitations of social structure were established before we are born. In other words, by the time any of us get here, most of the social structure governing our individual expression is in place and well entrenched.

It's easy to see why a society's need for structure and the individual's need for self-expression can conflict. Every person who wants to master the art of trading faces just such a fundamental conflict.

I'd like you to ask yourself what one characteristic (a form of personal expression) is common to every child born on this planet, regardless of the location, culture, or social situation the child is born into. The answer is curiosity. Every child is curious. Every child is eager to learn. They can be described as little learning machines.

Consider the nature of curiosity. At its most fundamental level, it is a force. More specifically, it is an inner-directed force, which means there's no necessity to motivate a child to learn something. Left on their own, children will naturally explore their surroundings. What is more, this inner-directed force also seems to have its own agenda; in other words, even though all children are curious, not all children are naturally curious about the same things.

There's something inside each of us that directs our awareness to certain objects and types of experiences to the exclusion of others.

Even infants seem to know what they want and don't want. When adults encounter this unique display of individuality expressed by an infant, they're usually surprised. They assume that infants have nothing inside of them that makes them uniquely who they are. How else would infants express their individuality than by what in their environment attracts or repels them? I call this inner-directed guidance the force of natural attractions.

Natural attractions are simply those things about which we feel a natural or passionate interest. Ours is a big and diverse world, and it offers each of us a great deal to learn about and experience. But that doesn't mean each of us has a natural or passionate interest in learning about or experiencing all there is. There's some internal mechanism that makes us "naturally selective."

If you think about it, I'm sure you could list many things to do or be that you have absolutely no interest in. I know I could. You could also make another list of the things you are only marginally interested in. Finally, you could list everything you have a passionate interest in. Of course, the lists get smaller as the interest levels rise.

Where does passionate interest come from? My personal view is that it comes from the deepest level of our being—at the level of our true identity. It comes from the part of us that exists beyond the characteristics and personality traits we acquire as a result of our social upbringing.

THE DANGERS

It is at the deepest level of our being that the potential for conflict exists. The social structure that we're born into may or may not be sensitive to these inner-directed needs and interests. For example, you may have been born into a family of extremely competitive athletes, but feel a passionate interest in classical music or art. You may even have natural athletic ability, but no real interest in participating in athletic events. Is there any potential for conflict here?

In a typical family, most members would put a great deal of pressure on you to follow in the footsteps of your brothers, sisters, or parents. They do everything possible to teach you their ways and how to get the most out of your athletic ability. They discourage you from seriously pursuing any other interests. You go along with what they want, because you don't want to be ostracized, but at the same time, doing what they want you to do just doesn't feel right, although everything you've learned and been taught argues in favor of becoming an athlete. The problem is, it doesn't feel like who you are.

The conflicts that result from what we're taught about who we're supposed to be and the feeling that resonates at the deepest levels of our being is not at all uncommon. I would say that many, if not most people, grow up in a family and cultural environment that gives little, if any, objective, nonjudgmental support to the unique ways in which we feel compelled to express ourselves.

This lack of support is not simply an absence of encouragement. It can be as deep as the outright denial of some particular way in which we want to express ourselves. For example, let's look at a common situation: A toddler, who for the first time in his life, notices "this thing," which we call a vase, on the coffee table. He is curious, which means there's an inner force that's compelling him to experience this object. In a sense, it's as if this force creates a vacuum in his mind that has to be filled with the object of his interest. So, he focuses on the vase, and, with deliberate intent, crawls across the vast expanse of the living room floor to the coffee table. When he gets there, he reaches up to the edge of the table to pull himself to his feet. With one hand firmly on the table to maintain his balance, his other hand reaches out to touch this thing he has never experienced. Just at that moment, he hears a scream from across the room, "NO! DON'T TOUCH THAT!"

Startled, the child falls back on his butt, and begins to cry. Obviously, this is a very common occurrence and one that is completely unavoidable. Children have absolutely no concept of how they can injure themselves or how valuable something like a vase can be. In fact, learning what is safe and what isn't and the value of things are important lessons the child must learn. However, there are some extremely important psychological dynamics at work here that have a direct effect on our ability to create the kind of discipline and focus necessary to trade effectively later in life.

What happens when we're denied the opportunity to express ourselves in the way we want to, or we're forced to express ourselves in a way that doesn't correspond with the natural selection process? The experience creates an upset. Being "up-set" implies an imbalance. But what exactly is out of balance? For something to be out of balance, there has to be something that's in balance or in equal proportion in the first place. That something is the relative degree of correspondence that exists between our inner, mental environment and the exterior environment where we experience our lives.

In other words, our needs and desires are generated in our mental environment, and they are fulfilled in the exterior environment . If these two environments are in correspondence with one another, we're in a state of inner balance and we feel a sense of satisfaction or happiness. If these environments are not in correspondence, we experience dissatisfaction, anger, and frustration, or what is commonly referred to as emotional pain.

Now, why would not getting what we want or being denied the freedom to express ourselves in some particular way cause us to experience emotional pain? My personal theory is that needs and desires create mental vacuums. The universe in which we live has a natural tendency to not tolerate a vacuum and moves to fill it, whenever one exists. (The philosopher Spinoza observed centuries ago that, "Nature abhors a vacuum.")

Suck the air out of a bottle and your tongue and lips will stick to the mouth of the bottle, because you have created an imbalance (a vacuum), which now must be filled. What are the dynamics behind the expression "Necessity is the mother of all invention"? The recognition that a need creates a mental vacuum that the universe will fill with inspiring thoughts (if your mind is receptive). The thoughts, in turn, can inspire movement and expression that result in the fulfillment of that need.

In this respect, I think our mental environment works like the universe at large. Once we recognize a need or desire, we move to fill the vacuum with an experience in the exterior environment. If we are denied the opportunity to pursue the object of this need or desire, it literally feels as if we are not whole, or that something is missing, which puts us into a state of imbalance or emotional pain. (Do our minds also abhor a vacuum, once one has been created?)

Take a toy away from a child who is not finished playing with it (regardless of how good your reasons may be for doing so) and the universal response will be emotional pain.

By the time we're 18 years old, we've been on Earth approximately 6,570 days. On average, how many times per day does the typical child hear statements like:

- "No, no, you can't do that."

- "You can't do it that way. You have to do it this way."

- "Not now; let me think about it."

- "I'll let you know."

- "It can't be done."

- "What makes you think you can do it?"

- "You have to do it. You have no choice."

These are just a few of the relatively nice ways in which all of us are denied individual expression as we grow up. Even if we only heard such statements once or twice a day, that still adds up to several thousand denials by the time we reach adulthood.

I call these kinds of experiences "denied impulses" to learn—impulses that are based on an inner need, originating from the deeper part of our identity, from the natural selection process.

What happens to all of these impulses that have been denied and left unfulfilled? Do they just go away? They can, if they are reconciled in some way: if we do something, or someone else does something, to put our mental environment back into balance. What can put our mental environment back into balance? There are a number of techniques. The most natural one, especially for a child, is simply to cry.

Crying is a natural mechanism (nature's way) for reconciling these denied, unfulfilled impulses. Scientific researchers have found tears to be composed of negatively charged ions. If allowed to take its natural course, crying will expel the negatively charged energy in our minds and bring us back to a state of balance, even though the original impulse was never fulfilled.

The problem is that, most of the time, events are not allowed to take their natural course and the denied impulses are never reconciled (at least, not while we're still children). There are many reasons why adults don't like it when their children (especially boys) cry, and do everything they can to discourage this behavior. There are just as many reasons why adults will not bother to explain to children why they are being forced to do something they don't want to do. Even if adults do try, there are no assurances that they will be effective enough to reconcile the imbalance. What happens if these impulses aren't reconciled?

They accumulate and usually end up manifesting themselves in any number of addictive and compulsive behavior patterns. A very loose rule of thumb is: Whatever we believe we were deprived of as children can easily become addictions in adulthood. For example, many people are addicted to attention. I am referring to people who will do most anything to draw attention to themselves. The most common reason for this is that they believe they either didn't get enough attention when they were young or didn't get it when it was important to them. In any case, the deprivation becomes unresolved emotional energy that compels them to behave in ways that will satisfy the addiction. What's important for us to understand about these unreconciled, denied impulses (that exist in all of us) is how they affect our ability to stay focused and take a disciplined, consistent approach to our trading.

THE SAFEGUARDS

To operate effectively in the trading environment, we need rules and boundaries to guide our behavior. It is a simple fact of trading that the potential exists to do enormous damage to ourselves—damage that can be way out of proportion to what we may think is possible. There are many kinds of trades in which the risk of loss is unlimited. To prevent the possibility of exposing ourselves to damage, we need to create an internal structure in the form of specialized mental discipline and a perspective that guides our behavior so that we always act in our own best interests. This structure has to exist within each of us, because unlike society, the market doesn't provide it.

The markets provide structure in the form of behavior patterns that indicate when an opportunity to buy or sell exists. But that's where the structure ends—with a simple indication. Otherwise, from each individual's perspective, there are no formalized rules to guide your behavior. There aren't even any beginnings, middles, or endings as there are in virtually every other activity we participate in.

This is an extremely important distinction with profound psychological implications. The market is like a stream that is in constant motion. It doesn't start, stop, or wait. Even when the markets are closed, prices are still in motion. There is no rule that the opening price on any day must be the same as the closing price the day before. Nothing we do in society properly prepares us to function effectively in such a "boundary-less" environment.

Even gambling games have built-in structures that make them much different from trading, and a lot less dangerous. For example, if we decide to play blackjack, the first thing we have to do is decide how much we are going to wager or risk. This is a choice we are forced to make by the rules of the game. If we don't make the choice, we don't get to play.

In trading, no one (except yourself) is going to force you to decide in advance what your risk is. In fact, what we have is a limitless environment, where virtually anything can happen at any moment and only the consistent winners define their risk in advance of putting on a trade. For everyone else, defining the risk in advance would force you to confront the reality that each trade has a probable outcome, meaning that it could be a loser. Consistent losers do almost anything to avoid accepting the reality that, no matter how good a trade looks, it could lose. Without the presence of an external structure forcing the typical trader to think otherwise, he is susceptible to any number of justifications, rationalizations, and the kind of distorted logic that will allow him to get into a trade believing that it can't lose, which makes determining the risk in advance irrelevant.

All gambling games have specified beginnings, middles, and endings, based on a sequence of events that determine the outcome of the game. Once you decide you are going to participate, you can't change your mind—you're in for the duration. That's not true of trading. In trading, prices are in constant motion, nothing begins until you decide it should, it lasts as long as you want, and it doesn't end until you want it to be over. Regardless of what you may have planned or wanted to do, any number of psychological factors can come into play, causing you to become distracted, change your mind, become scared or overconfident: in other words, causing you to behave in ways that are erratic and unintended.

Because gambling games have a formal ending, they force the participant to be an active loser. If you're on a losing streak, you can't keep on losing without making a conscious decision to do so. The end of each game causes the beginning of a new game, and you have to actively subject more of your assets to further risk by reaching into your wallet or pushing some chips to the center of the table.

Trading has no formal ending. The market will not take you out of a trade. Unless you have the appropriate mental structure to end a trade in a manner that is always in your best interest, you can become a passive loser. This means that, once you're in a losing trade, you don't have to do anything to keep on losing. You don't even have to watch. You can just ignore the situation, and the market will take everything you own—and more.

One of the many contradictions of trading is that it offers a gift and a curse at the same time. The gift is that, perhaps for the first time in our lives, we're in complete control of everything we do. The curse is that there are no external rules or boundaries to guide or structure our behavior. The unlimited characteristics of the trading environment require that we act with some degree of restraint and self-control, at least if we want to create some measure of consistent success. The structure we need to guide our behavior has to originate in your mind, as a conscious act of free will. This is where the many problems begin.

PROBLEM:
The Unwillingness to Create Rules

I have not yet encountered a person interested in trading who didn't resist the notion of creating a set of rules. The resistance isn't always overt. Quite the contrary, it's usually very subtle. We agree on the one hand that rules make sense, but we really have no intention of doing whatever is being suggested. This resistance can be intense, and it has a logical source.

Most of the structure in our minds was given to us as a result of our social upbringing and based on choices made by other people. In other words, it was instilled in our minds, but did not originate in our minds. This is a very important distinction. In the process of instilling structure, many of our natural impulses to move, express, and learn about the nature of our existence through our own direct experience were denied. Many of these denied impulses were never reconciled and still exist inside of us as frustration, anger, disappointment, guilt, or even hatred. The accumulation of these negative feelings acts as a force inside our mental environment causing us to resist anything that denies us the freedom to do and be whatever we want, when we want.

In other words, the very reason we are attracted to trading in the first place—the unlimited freedom of creative expression—is the same reason we feel a natural resistance to creating the kinds of rules and boundaries that can appropriately guide our behavior. It's as if we have found a Utopia in which there is complete freedom, and then someone taps us on the shoulder and says, "Hey, you have to create rules, and not only that, you also have to have the discipline to abide by them."

The need for rules may make perfect sense, but it can be difficult to generate the motivation to create these rules when we've been trying to break free of them most of our lives. It usually takes a great deal of pain and suffering to break down the source of our resistance to establishing and abiding by a trading regime that is organized, consistent, and reflects prudent money-management guidelines.

Now, I'm not implying that you have to reconcile all of your past frustrations and disappointments to become a successful trader, because that's not the case. And you certainly don't have to suffer. I've worked with many traders who have achieved their objectives of consistency and haven't done anything to reconcile their backlog of denied impulses. However, I am implying that you can't take for granted how much effort and focus you may have to put into building the kind of mental structure that compensates for the negative effect denied impulses can have on your ability to establish the skills that will assure your success as a trader.

PROBLEM:
Failure to Take Responsibility

Trading can be characterized as a pure, unencumbered personal choice with an immediate outcome. Remember, nothing happens until we decide to start; it lasts as long as we want; and it doesn't end until we decide to stop. All of these beginnings, middles, and endings are the result of our interpretation of the information available and how we choose to act on our interpretation. Now, we may want the freedom to make choices, but that doesn't mean we are ready and willing to accept the responsibility for the outcomes. Traders who are not ready to accept responsibility for the outcomes of their interpretations and actions will find themselves in a dilemma: How does one participate in an activity that allows complete freedom of choice, and at the same time avoid taking responsibility if the outcome of one's choices are unexpected and not to one's liking?

The hard reality of trading is that, if you want to create consistency, you have to start from the premise that no matter what the outcome, you are completely responsible. This is a level of responsibility few people have aspired to before they decide to become traders. The way to avoid responsibility is to adopt a trading style that is, to all intents and purposes, random. I define random trading as poorly-planned trades or trades that are not planned at all. It is an unorganized approach that takes into consideration an unlimited set of market variables, which do not allow you to find out what works on a consistent basis and what does not.

Randomness is unstructured freedom without responsibility. When we trade without well-defined plans and with an unlimited set of variables, it's very easy to take credit for the trades that turn out to our liking (because there was "some" method present). At the same time, it's very easy to avoid taking responsibility for the trades that didn't turn out the way we wanted (because there's always some variable we didn't know about and therefore couldn't take into consideration beforehand).

If the market's behavior were truly random, then it would be difficult if not impossible to create consistency. If it's impossible to be consistent, then we really don't have to take responsibility. The problem with this logic is that our direct experience of the markets tells us something different. The same behavior patterns present themselves over and over again. Even though the outcome of each individual pattern is random, the outcome of a series of patterns is consistent (statistically reliable). This is a paradox, but one that is easily resolved with a disciplined, organized, and consistent approach.

I've worked with countless traders who would spend hours doing market analysis and planning trades for the next day Then, instead of putting on the trades they planned, they did something else. The trades they did put on were usually ideas from friends or tips from brokers. I probably don't have to tell you that the trades they originally planned, but didn't act on, were usually the big winners of the day. This is a classic example of how we become susceptible to unstructured, random trading—because we want to avoid responsibility.

When we act on our own ideas, we put our creative abilities on the line and we get instant feedback on how well our ideas worked. It's very difficult to rationalize away any unsatisfactory results. On the other hand, when we enter an unplanned, random trade, it's much easier to shift the responsibility by blaming the friend or the broker for their bad ideas.

There's something else about the nature of trading that makes it easy to escape the responsibility that comes with creating structure in favor of trading randomly: It is the fact that any trade has the potential to be a winner, even a big winner. That big winning trade can come your way whether you are a great analyst or a lousy one; whether you do or don't take responsibility. It takes effort to create the kind of disciplined approach that is necessary to become a consistent winner. But, as you can see, it's very easy to avoid this kind of mental work in favor of trading with an undisciplined, random approach.

PROBLEM:
Addiction to Random Rewards

Several studies have been done on the psychological effects of random rewards on monkeys. For example, if you teach a monkey to do a task and consistently reward it every time the task is done, the monkey quickly learns to associate a specific outcome with the efforts. If you stop rewarding it for doing the task, within a very short period of time the monkey will simply stop doing the task. It won't waste its energy doing something that it has now learned it won't be rewarded for.

However, the monkey's response to being cut off from the reward is very different if you start out on a purely random schedule, instead of a consistent one. When you stop offering the reward, there's no way the monkey can know that it will never be rewarded again for doing that task. Every time it was rewarded in the past, the reward came as a surprise. As a result, from the monkey's perspective, there's no reason to quit doing the task. The monkey keeps on doing the task, even without being rewarded for doing it. Some will continue indefinitely.

I'm not sure why we're susceptible to becoming addicted to random rewards. If I had to guess, I would say that it probably has something to do with the euphoria-inducing chemicals that are released in our brains when we experience an unexpected, pleasant surprise. If a reward is random, we never know for sure if and when we might receive it, so expending energy and resources in the hope of experiencing that wonderful feeling of surprise again isn't difficult. In fact, for many people it can be very addicting. On the other hand, when we expect a particular outcome and it doesn't come about, we're disappointed and feel bad. If we do it again and get the same disappointing outcome, it isn't likely that we will keep doing something we know will cause us emotional pain.

The problem with any addiction is that it leaves us in a state of "choicelessness." To whatever degree the addiction dominates our state of mind, to that same degree our focus and efforts will be geared toward fulfilling the object of that addiction. Other possibilities that exist in any given moment to fulfill other needs (like the need to trust ourselves and not to subject too many of our assets to risk) are either ignored or dismissed. We feel powerless to act in any other way than to satisfy the addiction. An addiction to random rewards is particularly troublesome for traders, because it is another source of resistance to creating the kind of mental structure that produces consistency.

PROBLEM:
External versus Internal Control

Our upbringing has programmed us to function in a social environment, which means we've acquired certain thinking strategies for fulfilling our needs, wants and desires that are geared toward social interaction. Not only have we learned to depend on each other to fulfill the needs, wants and desires we cannot fulfill completely on our own, but in the process we've acquired many socially-based controlling and manipulating techniques for assuring that other people behave in a manner that is consistent with what we want.

The markets may seem like a social endeavor because there are so many people involved, but they're not. If, in today's modern society, we have learned to depend on each other to fulfill basic needs, then the market environment (even though it exists in the midst of modern society) can be characterized as a psychological wilderness, where it's truly every man or woman for himself or herself.

Not only can we not depend on the market to do anything for us, but it is extremely difficult, if not impossible, to manipulate or control anything that the market does. Now, if we've become effective at fulfilling our needs, wants and desires by learning how to control and manipulate our environment, but suddenly find ourselves, as traders, in an environment that does not know, care, or respond to anything that is important to us, where does that leave us? You're right if you said up the proverbial creek without a paddle.

One of the principal reasons so many successful people have failed miserably at trading is that their success is partly attributable to their superior ability to manipulate and control the social environment, to respond to what they want. To some degree, all of us have learned or developed techniques to make the external environment conform to our mental (interior) environment. The problem is that none of these techniques work with the market. The market doesn't respond to control and manipulation (unless you're a very large trader).

However, we can control our perception and interpretation of market information, as well as our own behavior. Instead of controlling our surroundings so they conform to our idea of the way things should be, we can learn to control ourselves. Then we can perceive information from the most objective perspective possible, and structure our mental environment so that we always behave in a manner that is in our own best interest.

CHAPTER 3

TAKING RESPONSIBILITY

Although the words "taking responsibility" sound simple, the concept is neither easy to grasp nor easy to put into practice in your trading. We have all heard the words and been confronted with the need to take responsibility so many times in our lives that it is easy to take for granted that we know exactly what the phrase means.

Taking responsibility in your trading and learning the appropriate principles of success are inextricably connected. You have to understand, with every fiber of your being, the ways in which you are and are not responsible for your success as a trader. Only then can you take on the characteristics that will allow you to join the select group of traders who are consistently successful in the markets.

At the end of Chapter 1, I introduced the idea of stepping into a future projection of yourself. In other words, the consistently successful trader that you want to become doesn't exist yet. You must create a new version of yourself, just as a sculptor creates a likeness of a model.

SHAPING YOUR MENTAL ENVIRONMENT

The tools you will use to create this new version of yourself are your willingness and desire to learn, fueled by your passion to be successful. If the willingness and desire to learn are your primary tools, then what is your medium? An artist creating a sculpture can choose to work in a number of mediums—clay, marble, or metal, for example—but if you want to create a new version of your personality that expresses itself as a consistently successful trader, you have only your beliefs and attitudes. The medium for your artistic endeavor will be your mental environment, where with your desire to learn, you can restructure and install the beliefs and attitudes that are necessary to achieve your ultimate goal.

I am assuming your ultimate goal is consistency. If you're like most traders, you don't realize the fullest potential of the opportunities available to you. To realize more and more of that potential, to make it more and more of a reality in your life, your primary goal has to be to learn how to think like a consistently successful trader.

Remember, the best traders think in a number of unique ways. They have acquired a mental structure that allows them to trade without fear and, at the same time, keeps them from becoming reckless and committing fear-based errors. This mind-set has a number of components, but the bottom line is that successful traders have virtually eliminated the effects of fear and recklessness from their trading. These two fundamental characteristics allow them to achieve consistent results.

When you acquire this mind-set, you, too, will be able to trade without fear. You will no longer be susceptible to the multitude of fear-based errors that come from rationalizing, subconsciously distorting information, hesitating, jumping the gun, or hoping. Once the fear is gone, there just won't be a reason to make these errors and, as a result, they will virtually disappear from your trading.

However, eliminating fear is only half the equation. The other half is the need to develop restraint. Excellent traders have learned that it is essential to have internal discipline or a mental mechanism to counteract the negative effects of euphoria or the overconfidence that comes from a string of winning trades. For a trader, winning is extremely dangerous if you haven't learned how to monitor and control yourself.

If we start from the premise that to create consistency traders must focus their efforts on developing a trader's mind-set, then it is easy to see why so many traders don't succeed. Instead of learning to think like traders, they think about how they can make more money by learning about the markets. It's almost impossible not to fall into this trap. There are a number of psychological factors that make it very easy to assume that it's what you don't know about the markets that causes your losses and lack of consistent results.

However, that's just not the case. The consistency you seek is in your mind, not in the markets. It's attitudes and beliefs about being wrong, losing money, and the tendency to become reckless, when you're feeling good, that cause most losses—not technique or market knowledge.

For example, if you could choose one of the following two traders to manage your money, which one would you pick? The first trader uses a simple, possibly even mediocre trading technique, but possesses a mind-set that is not susceptible to subconsciously distorting market information, hesitating, rationalizing, hoping, or jumping the gun. The second trader is a phenomenal analyst, but is still operating out of the typical fears that make him susceptible to all of the psychological maladies that the other trader is free of. The right choice should be obvious. The first trader is going to achieve far better results with your money.

Attitude produces better overall results than analysis or technique. Of course, the ideal situation is to have both, but you really don't need both, because if you have the right attitude—the right mind-set—then everything else about trading will be relatively easy, even simple, and certainly a lot more fun. I know for some of you this may be difficult to believe, or even distressing especially if you've been struggling for years to learn everything you can about the market.

Interestingly, most traders are closer to the way they need to think when they first begin trading than at any other time in their careers. Many people begin trading with a very unrealistic concept of the inherent dangers involved. This is particularly true if their first trade is a winner. Then they go into the second trade with little or no fear. If that trade is a winner, they go into the next trade with even less concern for what would otherwise be the unacceptable possibility of a loss. Each subsequent win convinces them that there is nothing to fear and that trading is the easiest possible way to make money.

This lack of fear translates into a carefree state of mind, similar to the state of mind many great athletes describe as a "zone." If you've ever had the occasion to experience the zone in some sport, then you know it is a state of mind in which there is absolutely no fear and you act and react instinctively. You don't weigh alternatives or consider consequences or second-guess yourself. You are in the moment and "just doing it." Whatever you do turns out to be exactly what needed to be done.

Most athletes never reach this level of play, because they never get past the fear of making a mistake. Athletes who reach the point where there is absolutely no fear of the consequences of screwing up will usually, and quite spontaneously, enter into "the zone." By the way, a psychological zone is not a condition you can will yourself into, the way you can will yourself into a feat of endurance. It is a state of mind you find yourself in that is inherently creative, and usually if you start thinking about your actions at a rational or conscious level, you pop right out of it.

Even though you cannot force or will yourself into a zone, you can set up the kind of mental conditions that are most conducive to experiencing "the zone," by developing a positive winning attitude. I define a positive winning attitude as expecting a positive result from your efforts, with an acceptance that whatever results you get are a perfect reflection of your level of development and what you need to learn to do better.

That's what the great athletes have: a winning attitude that allows them to easily move beyond their mistakes and keep going.

Others get bogged down in negative self-criticism, regret, and self-pity. Not many people ever develop a positive winning attitude. The curious anomaly of trading is that, if you start with a winning trade, you will automatically experience the kind of carefree mind-set that is a by-product of a winning attitude, without having developed the attitude itself. I know this may sound a bit confusing, but it has some profound implications.

If a few winning trades can cause you to enter into the kind of carefree state of mind that is an essential component to your success, but is not founded on the appropriate attitudes, then what you have is a prescription for extreme misunderstanding about the nature of trading that inevitably results in both emotional and financial disaster.

Putting on a few (or more) winning trades does not mean you have become a trader, but that's the way it feels, because it taps us into a state of mind that only the most accomplished people experience on a consistent basis. The fact is, you don't need the slightest bit of skill to put on a winning trade, and if it's possible to put on one winning trade without the slightest bit of skill, it is certainly possible to put on another and another. I know of several people who started their trading careers with fairly substantial strings of winning trades.

When you're feeling confident and unencumbered by fears and worries, it isn't difficult to put on a string of winning trades because it's easy to get into a flow, a kind of natural rhythm, where what you need to do seems obvious or self-evident. It's almost as if the market screams at you when to buy and when to sell, and you need very little in the way of analytical sophistication. And, of course, because you have no fear, you can execute your trades with no internal argument or conflict.

The point I am making is that winning in any endeavor is mostly a function of attitude. Many people are certainly aware of this, but at the same time, most people don't understand the significant part attitude plays in their results. In most sports or other competitive activities, participants must develop physical skills as well as mental skills in the form of strategies. If opponents are not evenly matched in the skills department, the one with superior skills usually (but not always) wins. When an underdog beats a superior opponent, what's the determining factor? When two opponents are evenly matched, what's the factor that tips the balance one way or the other? In both cases, the answer is attitude.

What makes trading so fascinating and, at the same time, difficult to learn is that you really don't need lots of skills; you just need a genuine winning attitude. Experiencing a few or more winning trades can make you feel like a winner, and that feeling is what sustains the winning streak. This is why it is possible for a novice trader to put on a string of winning trades, when many of the industry's best market analysts would give their right arms for a string of winning trades. The analysts have the skills, but they don't have the winning attitude. They're operating out of fear. The novice trader experiences the feeling of a winning attitude because he's not afraid. But that doesn't mean he has a winning attitude; it only means he hasn't experienced any pain from his trading activities to make him afraid.

REACTING TO LOSS

Eventually, our novice trader will experience a loss and being wrong, regardless of how positive he's feeling. Losing and being wrong are inevitable realities of trading. The most positive attitude imaginable coupled with the best analytical skills can't prevent a trader from eventually experiencing a losing trade. The markets are just too erratic and there are too many variables to consider for any trader to be right every time.

What happens when the novice trader finally does lose? What effect will it have on his carefree state of mind? The answers will depend on his expectations going into the trade and how he interprets the experience. And how he interprets the experience is a function of his beliefs and attitudes.

What if he is operating out of a belief that there's no possible way to avoid a loss, because losing is a natural consequence of trading—no different from, let's say, a restaurant owner incurring the expense of having to buy food? Furthermore, suppose that he has completely accepted the risk, meaning that he has considered and accounted for all of what would otherwise be the unacceptable possibilities in the market's behavior, both financially and emotionally. With these beliefs and expectations, it is unlikely that he would experience a deterioration of his attitude, and would simply go on to the next trade. By the way, this is an example of an ideal set of trading beliefs and attitudes.

Now suppose that he hasn't completely accepted the risk. What if his expectations didn't take into account any market behavior other than what he wanted? From this mental perspective, if the market doesn't do what he wants, he is going to feel pain—emotional pain. Expectations are our mental representations of how some future moment in the environment is going to look, sound, feel, smell, or taste. Depending upon how much energy is behind the expectation, it can hurt a lot when it isn't fulfilled.

Of the two different perspectives I just described, which one is likely to be held by our novice trader? The latter, of course. Only the very best traders have acquired the perspective described in the first scenario. And, as I indicated in Chapter 1, unless these very best traders grew up in successful trading families or had super traders for mentors (where appropriate attitudes about risk and loss were instilled in them from the very beginning of their careers), virtually every one of them had the common experience of losing one or more fortunes before they realized how they needed to think in order to be consistently successful.

It's a fundamental shift in attitude that accounts for their success, not some brilliant realization about the market, as most people erroneously assume. This erroneous assumption is prevalent among traders simply because very few of them really understand, at the deepest levels, just how critical a component attitude is in determining one's success.

We can safely assume that after a loss, our novice trader will be in a state of emotional pain. As a result, his trading will take on a whole new quality. He'll definitely lose that carefree state of mind, but more important, he will feel that the market did this to him: The market caused him to feel the pain he is experiencing; the market took away his winning feeling by subjecting him to a loss.

Notice how our trader is blaming the markets for losing or what he didn't get. Notice, too, how natural it is to feel the way he does. Think about how many times in our lives, especially as children, we were doing something we really enjoyed, like playing with a toy or with our friends, and someone with more power and authority forced us to stop what we were doing and do something we didn't want to do. All of us have lost things, had things taken away from us, been denied things we wanted or believed we deserved, been prevented from continuing an activity we were in the middle of, or been blocked from pursuing an idea we were passionate about.

The point is that in many of these situations, we did not need to take personal responsibility for what happened to us or for the pain we experienced, because we were powerless to do anything about it. We didn't choose to be forced out of a state of joy and happiness, into a state of emotional pain. The decision was out of our hands, against our will, and usually quite abrupt. Even though we may have been told we were responsible for what was happening to us, we may not have believed it or understood what it meant.

What's tangible, and what we can most easily relate to, is that we were having fun, and someone or something took us out of that fun and into pain. It wasn't our choice. The cause of our pain came to us from the outside; therefore, whatever force acted upon us in that moment was to blame. We learned not only that feeling good can instantly be replaced with feeling bad through no fault of our own; we also learned about betrayal. We felt betrayed because many of these situations were completely unexpected or unanticipated, meaning, we were unprepared for how some people in our lives had the potential to behave. If their behavior caused us to flip into a state of emotional pain, then we quite naturally would have felt betrayed.

As a side note, I feel it is important to say that many of our past, emotionally painful experiences were the result of well-meaning parents, teachers and friends, many of whom were only doing what they believed, at the time, was best for us. The best example is a child playing with a toy that is inherently dangerous. Take the toy away, and the child will cry to express the emotional pain he is experiencing, and, if we are dealing with a very young or immature child, in all likelihood he will not listen to anything reasonable that we say about why he cannot play with that toy.

But, at the same time, many people are born to immature and unreasonable parents, or encounter emotionally disturbed teachers, coaches, and employees who subconsciously or intentionally inflict their personal problems on anyone they perceive as having less power. What's even worse is many of the people who have a tendency toward victimizing others are also clever enough to do it in a way that makes their victims believe they caused their own pain. In any case, whether our painful experiences are the result of an act of love or intentionally inflicted is something each of us will have to determine for ourselves.

The bottom line is that, as adults when we get into a trading mode, we don't realize how natural it is to associate the instantaneous shift from joy to pain that we experienced so often as children with the same instantaneous shift from joy to pain that occurs when we trade. The implications are that if we haven't learned to accept the inherent risks of trading and don't know how to guard against making these natural connections between our past and the present, we will end up blaming the market for our results instead of taking responsibility for them.

Even though most people who trade consider themselves responsible adults, only the very best traders have reached a point where they can and do accept complete responsibility for the outcome of any particular trade. Everyone else to one degree or another assumes they are taking responsibility; but the reality is that they want the market to do it for them. The typical trader wants the market to fulfill his expectations, his hopes, and dreams.

Society may work this way but the markets certainly don't. In society, we can expect other people to behave in reasonable and responsible ways. When they don't, and if we suffer as a result, society makes remedies available to rectify the imbalance and make us whole again. The market, on the other hand, has no responsibility to give us anything or do anything that would benefit us. This may not be the way markets are advertised and certainly not the impression they want to project, but the reality is, every trader who participates in the markets does so for his own benefit. The only way one trader can benefit is if some other trader loses, whether the loss is in actual dollars as in a futures trade, or lost opportunity as in a stock trade.

When you put on a trade, it is in anticipation of making money. Every other trader in the world who puts on a trade does so for the same reason. When you look at your relationship with the market from this perspective, you could say that your purpose is to extract money from the markets, but, by the same token, the market's sole purpose is to extract money or opportunity from you.

If the market is a group of people interacting to extract money from one another, then what is the market's responsibility to the individual trader? It has no responsibility other than to follow the rules it has established to facilitate this activity. The point is, if you have ever found yourself blaming the market or feeling betrayed, then you have not given enough consideration to the implications of what it means to play a zero-sum game. Any degree of blaming means you have not accepted the reality that the market owes you nothing, regardless of what you want or think or how much effort you put into your trading.

In the market, typical social values of exchange do not come into play. If you don't understand this and find a way to reconcile the differences between the social norms you grew up with and the way the market works, you will continue to project your hopes, dreams, and desires onto the market believing it's going to do something for you. When it doesn't, you'll feel angry, frustrated, emotionally distraught, and betrayed.

Taking responsibility means acknowledging and accepting, at the deepest part of your identity, that *you*—not the market—are completely responsible for your success or failure as a trader. Granted, the market's purpose is to separate you from your money; but in the process of doing so, it also provides you with an endless stream of opportunities for you to take money from it. When prices move, that movement represents the collective actions of everyone participating at that moment. The market also generates information about itself, and makes it extremely easy to enter and exit trades (depending, of course, on the number of people participating).

From the individual's perspective, price movement, information, and the ability to enter and exit trades represent opportunities to see something and to act on what you perceive. During each moment the markets are open, you have an opportunity to enter a position, lighten up a position, add to a position, or exit a position. These are all opportunities to enrich yourself by taking profits or, at least, cutting your losses.

Let me pose a question. Do you feel responsible for fulfilling some other trader's expectations, hopes, dreams, and desires? Of course you don't. It sounds absurd to even ask. However, if you ever find yourself blaming the market and feeling betrayed, that is essentially what you are doing. You are expecting the collective actions of everyone participating in the market to make the market act in a way that gives you what you want. You have to learn for yourself how to get what you want out of the markets. The first major step in this learning process is taking complete and absolute responsibility.

Taking responsibility means believing that all of your outcomes are self-generated; that your results are based on your interpretations of market information, the decisions you make and the actions you take as a result. Taking anything less than complete responsibility sets up two major psychological obstacles that will block your success. First, you will establish an adversarial relationship with the market that takes you out of the constant flow of opportunities. Second, you will mislead yourself into believing that your trading problems and lack of success can be rectified through market analysis.

Let's consider the first obstacle. When you project any degree of responsibility onto the market for giving you money or cutting your losses, the market can all too easily take on the quality of an adversary or enemy. Losing (when you expected the market to do something different from what it did) will tap you into the same childlike feelings of pain, anger, resentment, and powerlessness that all of us felt when someone took something away from us, didn't give us what we wanted, or wouldn't let us do what we wanted.

No one likes to feel denied, especially if we believe that getting what we want will make us happy. In each of these situations, something or someone outside of us prevented us from expressing ourselves in some particular way. In other words, some outside force was acting against the inner force of our desires and expectations.

As a result, it feels natural to assign the market the power of an outside force that either gives or takes away. But consider the fact that the market presents its information from a neutral perspective. That means the market doesn't know what you want or expect, nor does it care, unless, of course, you trade the kind of position that can have a major impact on prices. Otherwise, each moment, each bid, and each offer gives you the opportunity to do something. You can put on a trade, take profits, or take off a loser. This is also true for those of you who are floor traders and are personally known to other floor traders, who may also know your position and, to your detriment, purposely take advantage of that knowledge. It just means that you have to be faster and more focused, or take whatever limitations you have in these areas into consideration and trade accordingly.

From the market's perspective, each moment is neutral; to you, the observer, every moment and price change can have meaning. But where do these meaning exist? The meanings are based on what you've learned, and exist inside your mind, not in the market. The market doesn't attach meanings or interpret the information it generates about itself (although there are always individuals who will offer an interpretation if you're willing to listen). Furthermore, the market doesn't know how you define an opportunity or a loss. The market doesn't know whether you perceive it as an endless stream of opportunities to enter and exit trades for both profits and losses at each and every moment, or whether you perceive it as a greedy monster ready and willing in any given moment to devour your money.

If you perceive the endless stream of opportunities to enter and exit trades without self-criticism and regret, then you will be in the best frame of mind to act in your own best interest and learn from your experiences. On the other hand, if what you perceive in market information is painful in some way, then you will naturally try to avoid that pain by either consciously or subconsciously blocking that information from your awareness. In the process of blocking that information, you'll systematically cut yourself off from any number of opportunities to enrich yourself. In other words, you cut yourself off from the opportunity flow

Furthermore, it will feel like the market is against you but only if you expect it to do something for you, or if you believe that it owes you something. If someone or something is against you and causes you pain, how are you likely to respond? You'll feel compelled to fight, but what exactly are you fighting? The market is certainly not fighting you. Yes, the market wants your money, but it also provides you with the opportunity to take as much as you can. Although it may feel as if you are fighting the market, or it is fighting you, the reality is you are simply fighting the negative consequences of not fully accepting that the market owes you nothing; and that you need to take advantage of the opportunities it presents by yourself, 100 percent and not one degree less.

The way to take maximum advantage of a situation where you are being offered unlimited opportunities to do something for yourself is to get into the flow. The market does have a flow. It is often erratic, especially in the shorter time frames, but it does display symmetrical patterns that repeat themselves over and over again. Obviously, it's a contradiction to flow with something you are against. If you want to start sensing the flow of the market, your mind has to be relatively free of fear, anger, regret, betrayal, despair, and disappointment. You won't have a reason to experience these negative emotions when you assume absolute responsibility.

Earlier, I said that when you don't take responsibility, one of the major psychological obstacles that can block your success is that you will mislead yourself into believing that your trading problems and lack of consistency can be rectified through market analysis. To illustrate this point, let's go back to our novice trader who started out with a carefree state of mind until he experienced his first loss.

After winning with such ease and effortlessness, the abrupt shift to emotional pain can be quite shocking—not shocking enough, however, to quit trading. Besides, in his mind the situation wasn't his fault anyway; the market did it to him. Instead of quitting, the great feeling that he experienced when he was winning will be fresh in his mind, and will inspire him with a sense of determination to continue trading.

Only now he's going to be smarter about it. He's going to put some effort into it and learn everything he can about the markets. It's perfectly logical to think that if he can win not knowing anything, he'll be able to clean up when he does know something. But there's a big problem here that very few, if any, traders will have any awareness of until long after the damage is done. Learning about the markets is fine and doesn't cause a problem in itself. It's the underlying reason for learning about the market that will ultimately prove to be his undoing.

As I said a moment ago, the sudden shift from joy to pain usually creates quite a psychological shock. Very few people ever learn how to reconcile these kinds of experiences in a healthy way. Techniques are available, but they aren't widely known. The typical response in most people, especially in the type of person attracted to trading, is revenge. For traders, the only way to extract that revenge is to conquer the market, and the only way to conquer the market is through market knowledge, or so they think. In other words, the underlying reason for why the novice trader is learning about the market is to overcome the market, to prove something to it and himself, and most important, to prevent the market from hurting him again. He is not learning the market simply as a means to give himself a systematic way of winning, but rather as a way to either avoid pain or prove something that has absolutely nothing to do with looking at the market from an objective perspective. He doesn't realize it, but as soon as he made the assumption that knowing something about the market can prevent him from experiencing pain or can help satisfy his desire for revenge or to prove something, he sealed his fate to become a loser.

In effect what he has done is set up an irreconcilable dilemma. He is learning how to recognize and understand the market's collective behavior patterns, and that's good. It even feels good. He's inspired because he assumes he's learning about the market in order to become a winner. As a result, he will typically go on a knowledge quest, learning about trend lines, chart patterns, support and resistance, candlesticks, market profiles, point and line charts, Elliott waves, Fibonacci retracements, oscillators, relative strength, stochastics, and many more technical tools too numerous to mention. Curiously, even though his knowledge has increased, he now finds that he's developed problems executing his trades. He hesitates, second-guesses himself, or doesn't put on a trade at all, in spite of any number of clear signals to do so. It's all frustrating, even maddening, because what's happened doesn't make sense. He did what he was supposed to do—he learned—only to find that the more he learned, the less he took advantage of. He would never believe that he did anything wrong by devoting himself to learning; he simply did it for the wrong reasons.

He won't be able to trade effectively if he is trying to prove something or anything for that matter. If you have to win, if you have to be right, if you can't lose or can't be wrong, you will cause yourself to define and perceive categories of market information as painful. In other words, you will view as painful any information the market generates that is in opposition to what will make you happy.

The dilemma is that our minds are wired to avoid both physical and emotional pain, and learning about the markets will not compensate for the negative effects our pain-avoidance mechanisms have on our trading. Everybody understands the nature of avoiding physical pain. Accidentally set your hand on a hot burner, and your hand moves away from the heat automatically; it's an instinctive reaction. However, when it comes to avoiding emotional pain and the negative consequences it creates, especially for traders, very few people understand the dynamics. It's absolutely essential to your development that you understand these negative effects and learn how to take conscious control in a way that helps you fulfill your goals.

Our minds have a number of ways to shield us from information that we have learned to perceive as painful. For example, at a conscious level, we can rationalize, justify, or make a case for staying in a losing trade. Some of the more typical ways we do this are to call our trading buddies, talk to our broker, or look at indicators we never use, all for the express purpose of gathering nonpainful information in order to deny the validity of the painful information. At a subconscious level, our minds will automatically alter, distort, or specifically exclude information from our conscious awareness. In other words, we don't know at a conscious level that our pain-avoidance mechanisms are either excluding or altering the information being offered by the market.

Consider the experience of being in a losing trade when the market is making consistently higher highs and higher lows or lower highs and lower lows against your position, while you refuse to acknowledge you are in a losing trade because you have focused all your attention on the tics that go in your favor. On the average, you are only getting one out of four or five tics in your direction; but it doesn't matter because every time you get one, you are convinced the market has reversed and is coming back. Instead the market keeps going against you. At some point, the dollar value of the loss becomes so great that it cannot be denied and you finally exit the trade.

The first reaction that traders universally have when looking back at such a trade is, "Why didn't I just take my loss and reverse?" The opportunity to put on a trade in the opposite direction was easily recognized once there was nothing at stake. But we were blinded to this opportunity while we were in the trade, because at that time the information indicating it was an opportunity was defined as painful, so we blocked it from our awareness.

When our hypothetical trader first started trading, he was having fun; he was in a carefree state of mind; he had no personal agendas and nothing to prove. As long as he was winning, he put his trades on from a "let's see what will happen" perspective. The more he won, the less he considered the possibility of ever losing. When he finally did lose, he was probably in a state of mind where he least expected it. Instead of assuming that the cause of his pain was his erroneous expectation about what the market was supposed to do or not do, he blamed the market, and resolved that by gaining market knowledge, he could prevent such experiences from recurring. In other words, he made a dramatic shift in his perspective from carefree to preventing pain by avoiding losses.

The problem is that preventing pain by avoiding losses can't be done. The market generates behavior patterns and the patterns repeat themselves, but not every time. So again, there is no possible way to avoid losing or being wrong. Our trader won't sense these trading realities, because he is being driven forward by two compelling forces: (1) he desperately wants that winning feeling back, and (2) he is extremely enthusiastic about all of the market knowledge he is acquiring. What he doesn't realize is that, in spite of his enthusiasm, when he went from a carefree state of mind to a prevent-and-avoid mode of thinking, he shifted from a positive to a negative attitude.

He's no longer focused on just winning, but rather on how he can avoid pain by preventing the market from hurting him again. This kind of negative perspective isn't any different from the tennis player or golfer who is focused on trying not to make a mistake, the more he tries not to make a mistake, the more mistakes he makes. However, this mode of thinking is much easier to recognize in sports because there's a more discernable connection between one's focus and one's results. With trading, the connection can be obscured and more difficult to recognize as a result of the positive feelings being generated from discovering new relationships in market data and behavior.

Since he is feeling good, there's no reason to suspect that anything is wrong, except that the degree to which his focus is weighted toward pain-avoidance is the same degree by which he will create the very experiences he is trying to avoid. In other words, the more he has to win and not lose, the less tolerance he will have for any information that might indicate he is not getting what he wants. The more information that he has the potential to block, the less he will be able to perceive an opportunity to act in his own best interests.

Learning more and more about the markets only to avoid pain will compound his problems because the more he learns, the more he will naturally expect from the markets, making it all the more painful when the markets don't do their part. He has unwittingly created a vicious cycle where the more he learns, the more debilitated he becomes; the more debilitated he becomes, the more he feel compelled to learn. The cycle will continue until he either quits trading in disgust or recognizes that the root cause of his trading problems is his perspective, not his lack of market knowledge.

WINNERS, LOSERS, BOOMERS, AND BUSTERS

It takes some time before most traders either throw in the towel or find out the true source of their success. In the meantime, some traders manage to get enough right about trading to enter into what is commonly referred to as the "boom and bust cycle."

Contrary to what some of you may have inferred from the example of the novice trader, not everyone has an inherently negative attitude and is therefore doomed to lose consistently. Yes, it is true that some traders do consistently lose, often until they lose everything or quit trading because they can't tolerate any more emotional pain. However, there are also many traders who are tenacious students of the market and have a sufficiently winning attitude going into trading so that, in spite of the many difficulties, they eventually learn how to make money. But, and I want to emphasize this, they learn how to make money only on a limited basis; they haven't yet learned how to counteract the negative effects of euphoria or how to compensate for the potential for self-sabotage.

Euphoria and self-sabotage are two powerful psychological forces that will have an extremely negative effect on your bottom line. But, they are not forces you have to concern yourself with until you start winning, or start winning on a consistent basis, and that's a big problem. When you're winning, you are least likely to concern yourself with anything that might be a potential problem, especially something that feels as good as euphoria. One of the primary characteristics of euphoria is that it creates a sense of supreme confidence where the possibility of anything going wrong is virtually inconceivable. Conversely, errors that result from self-sabotage have their root in any number of conflicts that traders have about deserving the money or deserving to win.

It's when you're winning that you are most susceptible to making a mistake, overtrading, putting on too large a position, violating your rules, or generally operating as if no prudent boundaries on your behavior are necessary. You may even go to the extreme of thinking you are the market. However, the market rarely agrees, and when it disagrees, you'll get hurt. The loss and the emotional pain are usually significant. You will experience a boom, followed by the inevitable bust.

If I were to classify traders based on the kind of results they achieve, I would put them into three broad categories. The smallest group, probably fewer than 10 percent of the active traders, are the consistent winners. They have a steadily rising equity curve with relatively minor drawdowns. The drawdowns they do experience are the type of normal losses that any trading methodology or system incurs. Not only have they learned how to make money, but they are no longer susceptible to the psychological forces that cause the boom-and-bust cycle.

The next group, which consists of between 30 and 40 percent of the active traders, are consistent losers. Their equity curves are mirror images of the consistent winners' curves, but in the opposite direction—many losing trades with an occasional winner. Regardless of how long they have been trading, there's much about it that they haven't learned. They either have illusions about the nature of trading or are addicted to it in ways that make it virtually impossible for them to be winners.

The largest group, the remaining 40 to 50 percent of the active traders, are the "boom and busters." They have learned how to make money, but they haven't learned there's a whole body of trading skills that have to be mastered in order to keep the money they make. As a result, their equity curves typically look like roller-coaster rides, with a nice, steady assent into a steep dropoff, then another nice, steady assent into another steep dropoff. The roller-coaster cycle continues on and on.

I have worked with many experienced traders who have put together incredible winning streaks, sometimes going months without a losing day; having fifteen or twenty winning trades in a row is not unusual for them. But for the boom and busters, these streaks always end the same way—in huge losses that are the result of either euphoria or self-sabotage.

If the losses are the result of euphoria, it really doesn't matter what form the streak takes—a number of wins in a row, a steadily rising equity curve, or even one winning trade. Everyone seems to have a different threshold for when overconfidence or euphoria starts to take hold of the thinking process. However, the moment euphoria takes hold, the trader is in deep trouble.

In a state of overconfidence or euphoria, you can't perceive any risk because euphoria makes you believe that absolutely nothing can go wrong. If nothing can go wrong, there's no need for rules or boundaries to govern your behavior. So putting on a larger than usual position is not only appealing, it's compelling.

However, as soon as you put on the larger-than-usual position, you're in danger. The larger the position, the greater the financial impact small fluctuations in price will have on your equity. Combine the larger-than-normal impact of a move against your position with a resolute belief that the market will do exactly as you expect, and you have a situation in which one tic in the opposition direction of your trade can cause you to go into a state of "mind-freeze" and become immobilized.

When you finally do pull yourself out of it, you'll be dazed, disillusioned, and betrayed, and you'll wonder how something like that could have happened. In fact, you were betrayed by your own emotions. However, if you're not aware of or don't understand the underlying dynamics I just described, you'll have no other choice but to blame the market. If you believe the market did this to you, then you'll feel compelled to learn more about the market in order to protect yourself. The more you learn, the more confident you will naturally become in your ability to win. As your confidence grows, the more likely that at some point you will cross the threshold into euphoria and start the cycle all over again.

Losses that result from self-sabotage can be just as damaging, but they're usually more subtle in nature. Making errors like putting in a sell for a buy or vice versa, or indulging yourself in some distracting activity at the most inopportune time are typical examples of how traders make sure they don't win.

Why wouldn't someone want to win? It's really not a question of what someone wants, because I believe that all traders want to win. Yet, there are often conflicts about winning. Sometimes these conflicts are so powerful that we find our behavior is in direct conflict with what we want. These conflicts could stem from religious upbringing, work ethic or certain types of childhood trauma.

If these conflicts exist, it means that your mental environment is not completely aligned with your goals. In other words, not all parts of you would argue for the same outcome. Therefore, you can't assume that you have the capacity to give yourself an unlimited amount of money just because you have learned how to trade and the money is there for the taking.

A futures broker at one of the major brokerage firms once commented that when it comes to his customers, he lives by the motto that all commodity traders are terminal, and it is his job to keep them happy until they're gone. He said this facetiously, but there is a lot of truth to his statement. Obviously, if you lose more money than you make, you can't survive. What's less obvious, and one of the mysteries of being successful, is that if you win, you may still be terminal; that is, if you win and you haven't learned how to create a healthy balance between confidence and restraint, or you haven't learned how to recognize and compensate for any potential you have to self-destruct, you will sooner or later lose.

If you are among those in the boom-and-bust cycle, consider this: If you could redo every losing trade that was the result of an error or recklessness, how much money would you have now? Based on these recalculated results, what would your equity curve look like? I'm sure many of you would fall into the category of consistent winners. Now think about how you responded to your losses when they occurred. Did you assume complete responsibility for them? Did you try to identify how you might change your perspective, attitude, or behavior? Or did you look to the market and wonder what you might learn about it to prevent such a thing from happening again? Obviously, the market has nothing to do with your potential for recklessness, nor does it have anything to do with the errors you make as a result of some internal conflict about deserving the money.

Probably one of the hardest concepts for traders to effectively assimilate is that the market doesn't create your attitude or state of mind; it simply acts as a mirror reflecting what's inside back to you. If you are confident, it's not because the market is making you feel that way; it is because your beliefs and attitudes are aligned in a way that allows you to step forward into an experience, take responsibility for the outcome, and extract the insight that's been made available. You maintain your confident state of mind simply because you are constantly learning. Conversely, if you're angry and afraid, it's because you believe to some degree that the market creates your outcomes, not the other way around.

Ultimately, the worst consequence of not taking responsibility is that it keeps you in a cycle of pain and dissatisfaction. Think about it for a moment. If you're not responsible for your results, then you can assume there's nothing for you to learn, and you can stay exactly as you are. You won't grow and you won't change. As a result, you will perceive events in exactly the same way, and therefore respond to them in the same way, and get the same dissatisfying results.

Or, you might also assume the solution to your problems is to gain more market knowledge. It is always virtuous to learn, but in this case if you don't take responsibility for your attitudes and perspective, then you're learning something valuable for the wrong reasons—reasons that will cause you to use what you've learned in inappropriate ways. Without realizing it, you'll be using your knowledge to avoid the responsibility of taking risks. In the process, you end up creating the very things you are trying to avoid, keeping you in a cycle of pain and dissatisfaction.

However, there is one tangible benefit to be gained from blaming the market for what you wanted and didn't get. You can temporarily shield yourself from your own harsh self-criticism. I say "temporarily" because, when you shift responsibility, you cut yourself off from whatever you needed to learn from the experience. Remember our definition of a winning attitude: a positive expectation of your efforts with an acceptance that whatever results you get are a perfect reflection of your level of development and what you need to learn to do better.

If you shift the blame in order to block the painful feelings that result from beating yourself up, all you've done is put an infected Band-Aid on the wound. You may think you have solved the problem, but the problem is only going to resurface later, worse than before. It has to, simply because you haven't learned anything that would cause you to make the kind of interpretations that would result in a more satisfying experience.

Did you ever wonder why leaving money on the table is often more painful than taking a loss? When we lose, there are any number of ways in which we can shift the blame to the market and not accept responsibility. But when we leave money on the table, we can't blame the market. The market didn't do anything but give us exactly what we wanted, but for whatever reason, we weren't capable of acting on the opportunity appropriately. In other words, there's no way to rationalize the pain away.

You are not responsible for what the market does or doesn't do, but you are responsible for everything else that results from your trading activities. You are responsible for what you have learned, as well as for everything you haven't learned yet that's waiting to be discovered by you. The most efficient path to discovering what you need to be successful is to develop a winning attitude, because it's an inherently creative perspective. Not only does a winning attitude open you up to what you need to learn; it also produces the kind of mind-set that is most conducive to discovering something no one else has experienced.

Developing a winning attitude is the key to your success. The problem for many traders is that either they think they already have one, when they don't, or they expect the market to develop the attitude for them by giving them winning trades. You are responsible for developing your own winning attitude. The market is not going to do it for you, and, I want to be as emphatic as I can, no amount of market analysis will compensate for developing a winning attitude if you lack one. Understanding the markets will give you the edge you need to create some winning trades, but your edge won't make you a consistent winner if you don't have a winning attitude.

Certainly one could argue that some traders lose because they don't understand enough about the markets and therefore they usually pick the wrong trades. As reasonable as this may sound, it has been my experience that traders with losing attitudes pick the wrong trades regardless of how much they know about the markets. In any case, the result is the same—they lose. On the other hand, traders with winning attitudes who know virtually nothing about the markets can pick winners; and if they know a lot about the markets, they can pick even more winners.

If you want to change your experience of the markets from fearful to confident, if you want to change your results from an erratic equity curve to a steadily rising one, the first step is to embrace the responsibility and stop expecting the market to give you anything or do anything for you. If you resolve from this point forward to do it all yourself, the market can no longer be your opponent. If you stop fighting the market, which in effect means you stop fighting yourself, you'll be amazed at how quickly you will recognize exactly what you need to learn, and how quickly you will learn it. Taking responsibility is the cornerstone of a winning attitude.

CHAPTER 4

CONSISTENCY:
A STATE OF MIND

I hope that after reading the first three chapters you are getting the idea that just because you are acting in the capacity of a trader, doesn't mean that you've learned the appropriate ways to think about what you do. As I have already stressed several times, what separates the best traders from everyone else is not what they do or when they do it, but rather how they think about what they do and how they're thinking when they do it.

If your goal is to trade like a professional and be a consistent winner, then you must start from the premise that the solutions are in your mind and not in the market. Consistency is a state of mind that has at its core certain fundamental thinking strategies that are unique to trading.

Experiencing a few or more winning trades can convince almost anyone that trading is easy. Recall your own experiences; think back to those trades that brought a stream of money flowing into your account when all you had done was make a simple decision to buy or sell. Now, combine the extremely positive feeling you get from winning and getting money with no effort, and it's almost impossible not to conclude that making money as a trader is easy.

But if that's the case, if trading is so easy, then why is it so difficult to master? Why are so many traders at their wits' end, grappling with the obvious contradiction? If it is true that trading is easy—and traders know it is because they've had the direct experience of how easy and effortless it is—then how can it also be possible that they can't make what they've learned about the markets work for them over and over again? In other words, how do we account for the contradiction between what we believe about trading and our actual trading results over time?

THINKING ABOUT TRADING

The answers are all in the way you think about it. The irony is that trading can be as much fun and as effortless as your experience of it has been on occasion; but experiencing these qualities consistently is a function of your perspective, your beliefs, your attitudes, or your mindset. Choose the term you are most comfortable with; they all refer to the same thing: Winning and consistency are states of mind in the same way that happiness, having fun, and satisfaction are states of mind.

Your state of mind is a by-product of your beliefs and attitudes. You can try to create consistency without having the appropriate beliefs and attitudes, but your results won't be any different than if you try to be happy when you're not having fun. When you're not having fun, it can be very difficult to change your perspective to one where you, all of a sudden, start enjoying yourself.

Of course, the circumstances of your situation could suddenly shift in a way that causes you to experience joy. But then your state of mind would be the result of an external shift in conditions, not a result of an internal shift in your attitude. If you depend on outside conditions and circumstances to make you happy (so that you always are enjoying yourself), then it is extremely unlikely that you will experience happiness on a consistent basis.

However, you can greatly increase the possibility of your being happy by developing fun-type attitudes and, more specifically, by working on neutralizing the beliefs and attitudes that prevent you from having fun or enjoying yourself. Creating consistent success as a trader works the same way. You can't rely on the market to make you consistently successful, any more than you can rely on the outside world to make you consistently happy. People who are truly happy don't have to do anything in order to be happy. They are happy people who do things.

Traders who are consistently successful are consistent as a natural expression of who they are. They don't have to try to be consistent; they are consistent. This may seem like an abstract distinction, but it is vitally important that you understand the difference. Being consistent is not something you can try to be, because the very act of trying will negate your intent by mentally taking you out of the opportunity flow, making it less likely that you will win and more likely you will lose.

Your very best trades were easy and effortless. You didn't have to try to make them easy; they were easy. There was no struggle. You saw exactly what you needed to see, and you acted on what you saw. You were in the moment, a part of the opportunity flow. When you're in the flow, you don't have to try, because everything you know about the market is available to you. Nothing is being blocked or hidden from your awareness, and your actions seem effortless because there's no struggle or resistance.

On the other hand, having to try indicates that there is some degree of resistance or struggle. Otherwise, you would just be doing it and not have to try to be doing it. It also indicates that you're trying to get what you want from the market. While it seems natural to think this way, it's a perspective fraught with difficulties. The best traders stay in the flow because they don't try to get anything from the market; they simply make themselves available so they can take advantage of whatever the market is offering at any given moment. There's a huge difference between the two perspectives.

In Chapter 3, I briefly illustrated how our minds are wired to avoid both physical and emotional pain. If you trade from the perspective of trying to get what you want or what you expect from the markets, what happens when the market doesn't behave in a way that will fulfill your expectations? Your mental defense mechanisms kick in to compensate for the difference between what you want and what you're not getting, so that you don't experience any emotional pain. Our minds are designed to automatically block threatening information or find a way to obscure that information, in order to shield us from the emotional discomfort we naturally feel when we don't get what we want. You won't realize it in the moment, but you will pick and choose information that is consistent with what you expect, so that you can maintain a pain-free state of mind.

However, in the process of trying to maintain a pain-free state of mind, you also take yourself out of the opportunity flow and enter the realm of the "could have," the "should have," the "would have," and the "if only." Everything that you could have, should have, or would have recognized in the moment appeared invisible, then all becomes painfully evident after the fact, after the opportunity is long gone.

To be consistent, you have to learn to think about trading in such a way that you're no longer susceptible to conscious or subconscious mental processes that cause you to obscure, block, or pick and choose information on the basis of what will make you happy, give you what you want, or avoid pain.

The threat of pain generates fear, and fear is the source of 95 percent of the errors you are likely to make. Certainly, you can't be consistent or experience the flow if you're consistently making errors, and you will make errors, as long as you're afraid that what you want or what you expect won't happen. Furthermore, everything you attempt to do as a trader will be a struggle, and it will seem as if you are struggling against the market or that the market is against you personally. But, the reality is that it's all taking place inside your mind. The market doesn't perceive the information it makes available; you do. If there's a struggle, it is you who are struggling against your own internal resistance, conflicts, and fears.

Now, you may be asking yourself, how can I think about trading in such a way that I'm no longer afraid and, therefore, no longer susceptible to the mental processes that cause me to block, obscure, or pick and choose information? The answer is: Learn to accept the risk.

REALLY UNDERSTANDING RISK

Other than the many issues surrounding responsibility that we discussed in Chapter 3, there isn't anything about trading that is more central to your success and also more misunderstood than the concept of accepting the risk. As I mentioned in the first chapter, most traders erroneously assume that because they are engaged in the inherently risky activity of putting on and taking off trades, they are also accepting that risk. I will repeat that this assumption couldn't be further from the truth.

Accepting the risk means accepting the consequences of your trades without emotional discomfort or fear. This means that you must learn how to think about trading and your relationship with the markets in such a way that the possibility of being wrong, losing, missing out, or leaving money on the table doesn't cause your mental defense mechanisms to kick in and take you out of the opportunity flow. It doesn't do you any good to take the risk of putting on a trade if you are afraid of the consequences, because your fears will act on your perception of information and your behavior in a way that will cause you to create the very experience you fear the most, the one you are trying to avoid.

I am offering you a specific thinking strategy composed of a set of beliefs that will keep you focused, in the moment, and in the flow. With this perspective, you will not be trying to get anything from the market or to avoid anything. Rather, you will let the market unfold and you will make yourself available to take advantage of whatever situations you define as opportunities.

When you make yourself available to take advantage of an opportunity, you don't impose any limitations or expectations on the market's behavior. You are perfectly satisfied to let the market do whatever it's going to do. However, in the process of doing something, the market will create certain conditions you define and perceive as opportunities. You act on those opportunities to the best of your ability, but your state of mind is not dependent upon or affected by the market's behavior.

If you can learn to create a state of mind that is not affected by the market's behavior, the struggle will cease to exist. When the internal struggle ends, everything becomes easy. At that point, you can take full advantage of all your skills, analytical or otherwise, to eventually realize your potential as a trader.

Here's the challenge! How do you accept the risks of trading without emotional discomfort and fear, when at the moment you perceive the risk, you simultaneously feel discomfort and fear? In other words, how do you remain confident and pain-free when you are absolutely certain you can be proved wrong, lose money, miss out, or leave money on the table? As you can see, your fear and feeling of discomfort are completely justified and rational. Each of those possibilities becomes real the moment you contemplate interacting with the market.

However, as true as all of these possibilities are for every trader, what isn't true or the same for every trader is what it means to be wrong, lose, miss out, or leave money on the table. Not everyone shares the same beliefs and attitudes about these possibilities and, therefore, we don't share the same emotional sensitivities. In other words, not everyone is afraid of the same things. This may seem obvious, but I assure you it is not. When we're afraid, the emotional discomfort we feel in the moment is so real that it's beyond question, and it's natural to assume that everyone shares our reality.

I will give you a perfect example of what I am talking about. I recently worked with a trader, who was deathly afraid of snakes. As far as he was concerned, he had always been afraid of snakes because he couldn't recall a time when he wasn't. Now he is married and has a three-year-old daughter. One evening, while his wife was out of town, his daughter and he were invited to a friend's house for dinner. Unbeknownst to my client, his friend's child had a pet snake.

When the friend's child brought out the snake for everyone to see, my client freaked and practically leapt to the other side of the room to get as far away from the snake as possible. His daughter, on the other hand, was completely enthralled with the snake, and wouldn't leave it alone.

When he related this story to me, he said that he was not only shocked by the unexpected confrontation with the snake, but that he was just as shocked by his daughter's reaction. She wasn't afraid and he assumed that she would be. I explained to him that his fear was so intense and his attachment to his daughter was so great that it was inconceivable to him that his daughter would not automatically share his reality about snakes. But then I pointed out, there really wasn't any way she could have shared his experience, unless he specifically taught her to be afraid of snakes or she had had her own painful frightening experience. Otherwise, without anything to the contrary in her mental system, the most likely reaction to her first encounter with a living snake would be pure, unadulterated fascination.

Just as my client assumed that his daughter would be afraid of snakes, most traders assume the best traders, like themselves, are also afraid of being wrong, losing, missing out, and leaving money on the table. They assume that the best traders somehow neutralize their fears with an inordinate amount of courage, nerves of steel, and self-control.

Like many other things about trading, what seems to make sense, just isn't the case. Certainly, any one or all of these characteristics may be present in any top trader. But what is not true is that these characteristics play any role in their superior performance. Needing courage, nerves of steel, or self-control would imply an internal conflict where one force is being used to counteract the effects of another. Any degree of struggle, trying, or fear associated with trading will take you out of the moment and flow and, therefore, diminish your results.

This is where professional traders really separate themselves from the crowd. When you accept the risk the way the pros do, you won't perceive anything that the market can do as threatening. If nothing is threatening, there's nothing to fear. If you're not afraid, you don't need courage. If you're not stressed, why would you need nerves of steel? And if you're not afraid of your potential to get reckless, because you have the appropriate monitoring mechanisms in place, then you have no need for self-control. As you contemplate the implications of what I am saying, I want you to keep something in mind: Very few people who go into trading start out with the appropriate beliefs and attitudes about responsibility and risk. There are some who do but it's rare. Everyone else goes through the same cycle I described in the example of the novice trader: We start out carefree, then become scared, and our fears continually diminish our potential.

The traders who break through the cycle and ultimately make it are the ones who eventually learn to stop avoiding and start embracing the responsibility and the risk. Most of those who successfully break the cycle don't make the shift in thinking until they have experienced so much pain from large losses that it has the positive effect of stripping away their illusions about the nature of trading.

With respect to your development, the *how* of their transformation is not that important, because in most cases it happened inadvertently. In other words, they weren't completely aware of the shifts that were taking place inside their mental environment until they experienced the positive effects their new perspective had on the ways in which they interacted with the market. This is why very few top traders can really explain what accounts for their success, except to speak in axioms like "cut your losses" and "go with the flow." What is important is that you understand it is completely possible to think the way the professionals do and to trade without fear, even though your direct experience as a trader would argue otherwise.

ALIGNING YOUR MENTAL ENVIRONMENT

Now we're going to start zeroing in on exactly how you can align your mental environment in order to accept the risk and function like a professional trader. Most of what I've discussed up to this point was designed to get you ready to do the real work. I'm going to teach you a thinking strategy that has, at its core, a firm belief in probabilities and edges. With this new thinking strategy, you'll learn how to create a new relationship with the market, one that disassociates your trading from what it typically means to be wrong or to lose, and that precludes you from perceiving anything about the market as threatening. When the threat of pain is gone, the fear will correspondingly disappear, as will the fear-based errors you are susceptible to. You will be left with a mind that is free to see what is available and to act on what you see.

Getting to this carefree, fearless state of mind, in spite of being burned over and over again, will take some work, but it's not going to be so difficult as you may think. In fact, by the time you've finished reading this book, most of you will be amazed at how simple the solutions to your problems really are.

In many respects, a state of mind or perspective is like software code. You could have several thousand lines of perfectly written code, with only one flawed line, and in that one flawed line there might be only one character out of place. Depending on the purpose of the software and where that flaw is in relation to everything else, that one misplaced character could ruin the performance of an otherwise perfectly written system. You see, the solution was simple: Fix the misplaced character, and everything runs smoothly. However, finding the error or even knowing it exists in the first place can take considerable expertise.

When it comes to the ideal trading mentality, everybody is a certain psychological distance away. In other words, virtually everyone starts out with flawed software code. I use terms like clicks or degrees to indicate psychological distance but these terms don't imply a specific distance. So, for example, many of you will find that you are only, let's say, one click away in perspective from the ideal mind-set. That one click could represent one or two erroneous or misplaced assumptions you have about the nature of trading. As you reflect upon some of the ideas presented in this book, your perspective may shift. To use the analogy of software code, that shift would be equivalent to finding the flawed line in your mental system and replacing it with something that works properly.

People normally describe this kind of internal mental shift as an "ah, ha" experience, or the moment when the light goes on. Everyone has had these kinds of experiences, and there are some common qualities associated with them. First, we usually feel different. The world even seems different, as if it had suddenly changed. Typically, we might say at the moment of the breakthrough something like, "Why didn't you tell me this before?" or, "It was right in front of me the whole time, but I just didn't see it" or, "It's so simple; why couldn't I see it?" Another interesting phenomenon of the "ah, ha" experience, is that sometimes within moments, although the amount of time can vary, we feel as if this new part of our identity has always been a part of who we are. It then becomes difficult to believe that we were ever the way we were before we had the experience.

In short, you may already have some awareness of much of what you need to know to be a consistently successful trader. But being aware of something doesn't automatically make it a functional part of who you are. Awareness is not necessarily a belief. You can't assume that learning about something new and agreeing with it is the same as believing it at a level where you can act on it.

Take the example of my client who is afraid of snakes. He is certainly aware that not all snakes are dangerous, and that learning how to make a distinction between the ones that are dangerous and the ones that aren't would not be difficult. Will learning how to make these distinctions suddenly cause him not to be afraid of "non-dangerous snakes"? Can we assume that his awareness will drop down to a level in his mental environment where he can now interact with snakes without fear or immobility? No, we cannot make this assumption. His awareness that some snakes aren't dangerous and his fear of snakes can exist side by side in his mental environment, as a contradiction to each other. You could confront him with a snake and he might readily acknowledge that he knows the snake is not dangerous and wouldn't hurt him; but, at the same time, he would still find it extremely difficult to touch the snake, even if he wanted to.

Does this mean that he is doomed to be afraid of snakes for the rest of his life? Only if he wants to be. It's really a matter of willingness. It's certainly possible to neutralize his fear, but he will have to work at it, and working at anything requires sufficient motivation. Many of us have what we know to be irrational fears and simply choose to live with the contradiction because we don't want to go through the emotional work that is necessary to overcome the fear.

In this example, the contradiction is obvious. However, in my many years of working with traders, I have uncovered several typical contradictions and conflicts surrounding the issues of risk and responsibility, where holding two or more conflicting beliefs can easily cancel out your positive intentions, no matter how motivated you are to be successful. The problem is that none of these contradictions are really obvious, at least not at first glance.

Contradictory beliefs, however, aren't the only problems. What about assertions like "I'm a risk taker," that traders typically assume have dropped down to the functional level of a belief when, in fact, the underlying dynamics of the way they perceive the market indicates they are doing everything possible to avoid risk.

Contradictory beliefs and nonfunctional awareness represent flawed mental software code; code that destroys your ability to stay focused and accomplish your goals; code that makes it seem as if you simultaneously have one foot on the accelerator and the other on the brake; code that gives learning how to trade a mysterious quality that will be challenging in a fun way at first, but usually turns into pure, unadulterated exasperation.

When I was in college in the late 1960s, one of my favorite movies was *Cool Hand Luke*, starring Paul Newman. It was a very popular movie back then, so I'm sure some of you have seen it on late-night TV. Luke was in a Georgia chain gang. After he escaped and was caught for the second time, the warden and guards were determined not to let Luke make fools of them a third time. So while forcing him to do an inordinate amount of work with no rest and giving him intermittent beatings, they kept asking, "Have you got your mind right yet, Luke?" Eventually, after considerable suffering, Luke finally told the prison bosses that he had his mind right. They said that if he didn't, and tried to escape again, they'd kill him for sure. Of course, Luke attempted another escape, and true to their word, the guards killed him.

Like Luke, many traders, whether they realize it or not, are trying to have it their way by beating the market; as a result, they get financially and emotionally killed. There are easier, infinitely more satisfying ways of getting what you want from the market, but first you have to be willing to "get your mind right."

CHAPTER 5

THE DYNAMICS OF PERCEPTION

One of the primary objectives of this book is to teach you how to take the threat of pain out of market information. The market doesn't generate happy or painful information. From the market's perspective, it's all simply information. It may seem as if the market is causing you to feel the way you do at any given moment, but that's not the case. It's your own mental framework that determines how you perceive the information, how you feel, and, as a result, whether or not you are in the most conducive state of mind to spontaneously enter the flow and take advantage of whatever the market is offering.

Professionals don't perceive anything about the markets as painful; therefore, no threat exists for them. If there's no threat, there's nothing to defend against. As a result, there isn't any reason for their conscious or subconscious defense mechanisms to kick in. That's why professionals can see and do things that mystify everyone else. They're in the flow, because they're perceiving an endless stream of opportunities, and when they're not in the flow, the very best of the best can recognize that fact and then compensate by either scaling back or not trading at all.

If your goal is to be able to trade like the professionals, you must be able to see the market from an objective perspective, without distortion. You must be able to act without resistance or hesitation, but with the appropriate amount of positive restraint to counteract the negative effects of overconfidence or euphoria. In essence, your objective is to be able to create a unique state of mind, a trader's mentality. When you've accomplished this, everything else about your success as a trader will fall into place.

To help you achieve that objective, I'm going to give you a way to redefine your relationship to market information so that there will be little or no potential to perceive any of it as threatening. By "redefine," I mean to change your perspective and operate out of a mental framework that keeps you focused on the opportunities available instead of tapping you into emotional pain.

DEBUGGING YOUR MENTAL SOFTWARE

In other words, we want to get the bugs out of our mental software code and get our minds right. Doing this effectively will require an understanding of the nature of mental energy and how you can use that energy to change a perspective that is generating an unwanted, negative, emotional response to market information. There's much to learn, but I think you will be amazed at how some simple changes can make a huge difference in your trading results.

The process of trading starts with perceiving an opportunity. Without the perception of an opportunity, we wouldn't have a reason to trade. So I think it is only fitting that we start our examination of mental energy by breaking down the process of perception. What are the underlying dynamics of perception? What factors determine how we perceive information or what we perceive in relationship to what is available? How is perception connected with what we experience at any given moment?

Probably the easiest way to understand the dynamics of perception and answer these questions is to think of everything (and I do mean everything) that exists in, on, and around this planet as a collection of forces—forces that generate information about the properties, characteristics, and traits that make them uniquely what they are.

Everything that exists outside of our bodies—all plants and all categories of life; all planetary phenomena in the form of weather conditions, earthquakes, and volcanic eruptions; all active and inert physical matter; and all noncorporeal phenomena such as light, sound waves, microwaves, and radiation—generates information about the nature of its existence. That information has the potential to act as a force on one of our five physical senses.

Before we go any further, notice that I use the verb "generate" in an all-inclusive way, implying that everything is in an active state of expression, including inanimate objects. To illustrate why I do that, let's look at something as simple as a rock. It's an inanimate object, composed of unique atoms and molecules expressing themselves as a rock. I can use the active verb "expressing" because the atoms and molecules that make up the rock are in constant motion. So, even though the rock doesn't appear active except in the most abstract sense, it has characteristics and properties that will act as forces on our senses, causing us to experience and make distinctions about the nature of its existence. For example, a rock has texture, and that texture acts as a force on our sense of touch if we run our fingers across the rock's surface. A rock has shape and color, which act as a force on our vision; the rock takes up space that no other object can occupy, so that we see it instead of an empty space or some other object. A rock can also have an odor that acts as a force on our sense of smell, or taste like something, although I haven't licked any rocks lately to find out.

When we encounter anything in the environment that express-es its properties and characteristics, an exchange of energy takes place. Energy from the outside, in the form of whatever is expressing itself, gets transformed by our nervous system into electrical impuls-es and then gets stored in our inner, mental environment. To be more specific, whatever we are seeing, hearing, tasting, smelling, or feeling through our senses gets transformed into electrical impulses of ener-gy and stored in our mental environment as a memory and/or dis-tinction about the nature of the way things exist.

I think all of this is fairly self-evident to most people, but there are some profound implications here that aren't self-evident, and we typically take them completely for granted. First of all, there's a cause-and-effect relationship that exists between ourselves and everything else that exists in the external environment. As a result, our encounters with external forces create what I am going to call "energy structures" inside our minds. The memories, distinctions, and, ultimately, the beliefs we acquire throughout our lives exist in our mental environment in the form of structured energy. Structured energy is an abstract concept. You might be asking yourself, "How does energy take shape or form?" Before I answer this question, an even more fundamental question needs to be addressed. How do we know that memories, distinctions, and beliefs exist in the form of energy in the first place?

I don't know if it's been scientifically proven or completely accepted by the scientific community, but ask yourself in what other form could these mental components exist? Here's what we know for sure: Anything composed of atoms and molecules takes up space and, therefore, can be observed. If memories, distinctions, and beliefs existed in some physical form, then we should be able to observe them. To my knowledge, no such observations have been made. The scientific community has dissected brain tissue (both living and dead) examined it at the level of the individual atom, mapped various regions of the brain in terms of their functions, but nobody, as yet, has *observed* a memory, distinction, or belief in its natural form. By "in its natural form" I mean that although a scientist can observe the individual brain cells that contain certain memories, he can't experience those memories first hand. He can only experience them if the person to whom the memories belong is alive and chooses to express them in some way.

If memories, distinctions, and beliefs don't exist as physical matter, then there really isn't any alternative way for them to exist except as some form of energy. If this is in fact the case, can this energy take on a specific shape? Can it be structured in a way that reflects the external forces that caused it to come into existence? Most definitely! Is there anything in the environment that is analogous to energy having shape or a specific structure? Yes! Let me give you several examples.

Thoughts are energy. Because you think in a language, your thoughts are structured by the limitations and rules that govern the particular language in which you think. When you express those thoughts aloud, you create sound waves, which are a form of energy. The sound waves created by the interaction of your vocal cords and tongue are structured by the content of your message. Microwaves are energy. Many phone calls are relayed by microwaves, which means that the microwave energy has to be structured in a way that reflects the message it is carrying. Laser light is energy, and if you've ever witnessed a demonstration of a laser light show, or laser art, what you've seen is pure energy taking a shape that reflects the creative desires of the artists.

All of these are good examples of how energy can take shape, form, and structure. Of course, there are many more, but there is one more example that illustrates the point in the most graphic way. At the most fundamental level, what are dreams? I am not asking you what dreams mean or what you think their purpose is, but rather, what are they? What are their properties? If we assume that dreams take place within the confines of our skulls, then they can't be composed of atoms and molecules, because there wouldn't be enough space for all of the things that exist and take place in our dreams. Dream experiences seem to have the same proportions and dimensions as the things we perceive when we are awake and experiencing life through our five senses. The only way this could be possible is if dreams were a form of structured energy, because energy can take on any size or dimension, but, in doing so, doesn't actually take up any space.

Now, if it hasn't already occurred to you, there's something here that's really profound. If the memories, distinctions, and beliefs we've acquired as a result of our encounters with the external environment represent what we've learned about that environment and how it works; and if these memories, distinctions, and beliefs exist in our mental environment as energy; and if energy doesn't take up any space; then it also could be said that we have an unlimited capacity for learning. Well, not only do I think it could be said, I'm saying it.

Consider the development of human consciousness and what we've learned collectively, as well as what the typical individual needs to know to function effectively compared to just 100 years ago. There is absolutely nothing to indicate that we don't have an unlimited capacity to learn. The difference between what we are aware of now and what we can do as a result of this expanded awareness would boggle the mind of anyone living 100 years ago.

PERCEPTION AND LEARNING

However, we must be careful not to equate storage capacity with learning capacity. Learning, and becoming aware of what is available to be learned, is not just a function of storage capacity. If it were, then what would stop us from knowing everything? And if we knew everything, then what would stop us from perceiving every possible characteristic, property, or trait of everything that is expressing itself in any given moment? What stops us now?

These questions get to the very heart of why you have to understand that mental components like memories, distinctions, and beliefs exist as energy. Anything that is energy has the potential to act as a force expressing its form, and that is exactly what our memories, distinctions and beliefs do. They act as a force on our senses from the inside, expressing their form and content, and, in the process of doing so, they have a profoundly limiting effect on the information we perceive in any given moment, making much of the information that is available from the environment's perspective, and the possibilities inherent within that information, literally invisible.

I am saying here that, in any given moment the environment is generating an enormous amount of information about its properties, characteristics, and traits. Some of that information is beyond the physiological range of our senses. For example, our eyes can't see every wavelength of light nor can our ears hear every frequency of sound the environment produces, so there's definitely a range of information that is beyond the physiological capabilities of our senses.

What about the rest of the information the environment is generating about itself? Do we see, hear, taste, smell, or feel through our senses every possible distinction, trait, and characteristic being expressed by everything that is within the physiological range of our senses? Absolutely not! The energy that's inside of us will categorically limit and block our awareness of much of this information by working through the same sensory mechanisms the external environment works through.

Now, if you take a moment and think about it, some of what I just said should be self-evident. For example, there are many ways in which the external environment can express itself that we don't perceive simply because we haven't learned about them yet. This is easy to illustrate. Think back to the first time you ever looked at a price chart. What did you see? Exactly what did you perceive? With no previous exposure, I'm sure, like everyone else, you saw a bunch of lines that had no meaning. Now if you're like most traders, when you look at a price chart you see characteristics, traits, and behavior patterns that represent the collective actions of all the traders who participated in those particular trades.

Initially, the chart represented undifferentiated information. Undifferentiated information usually creates a state of confusion, and that's probably what you experienced when you first encountered a chart. Gradually, however, you learned to make distinctions about that information, such as trends and trend lines, consolidations, support and resistance, retracements or significant relationships between volume, and open interest and price action, just to name a few. You learned that each of these distinctions in the market's behavior represented an opportunity to fulfill some personal need, goal, or desire. Each distinction now had a meaning and some relative degree of significance or importance attached to it.

Now, I want you to use your imagination and pretend that I just set before you the very first price chart you ever saw. Would there be a difference between what you see now and what you saw then? Absolutely. Instead of a bunch of undifferentiated lines, you would see everything you've learned about those lines between then and now. In other words, you would see all the distinctions you've learned to make, as well as all the opportunities those distinctions represent.

Yet, everything you can see as you look at that chart now existed then, and, furthermore, was available to be perceived. What's the difference? The structured energy that's inside of you now—the knowledge you have gained—acts as a force on your eyes, causing you to recognize the various distinctions that you've learned about. Since that energy wasn't there the first time you looked at the chart, all the opportunities that you now see were there, but at the same time invisible to you. Furthermore, unless you've learned to make every possible distinction based on every possible relationship between the variables in that chart, what you haven't learned yet is still invisible.

Most of us have no concept of the extent to which we are continually surrounded by the invisible opportunities inherent in the information we're exposed to. More often than not, we never learn about these opportunities and, as a result, they remain invisible. The problem, of course, is that unless we're in a completely new or unique situation or we're operating out of an attitude of genuine openness, we won't perceive something that we haven't learned about yet. To learn about something, we have to be able to experience it in some way. So what we have here is a closed loop that prevents us from learning. Perceptual closed loops exist in all of us, because they are natural functions of the way mental energy expresses itself on our senses.

Everyone has heard the expression, "People see what they want to see." I would put it a little differently: People see what they've learned to see, and everything else is invisible until they learn how to counteract the energy that blocks their awareness of whatever is unlearned and waiting to be discovered.

To illustrate this concept and make it even clearer, I am going to give you another example, one that demonstrates how mental energy can affect how we perceive and experience the environment in a way that it actually reverses the cause-and-effect relationship. Let's look at a very young child's first encounter with a dog.

Because it's a first-time experience, the child's mental environment is a clean slate, so to speak, with respect to dogs. He won't have any memories and certainly no distinctions about a dog's nature. Therefore, up to the moment of his first encounter, from the child's perspective, dogs don't exist. Of course, from the environment's perspective, dogs do exist and they have the potential to act as a force on the child's senses to create an experience. In other words, dogs expressing their nature can act as a cause to produce an effect inside the child's mental environment.

What kind of effect are dogs capable of producing? Well, dogs have a range of expression. By range of expression I mean dogs can behave in a number of ways toward humans. They can be friendly, loving, protective, and fun to play with; or they can be hostile, mean, and dangerous—just to name a few of the many behaviors they're capable of. All of these traits can be observed, experienced, and learned about. When the child sees the dog for the first time, there is absolutely nothing in his mental environment to tell him what he is dealing with. Unfamiliar, unknown, and unclassified environmental information can generate a sense of curiosity—when we want to find out more about what we're experiencing—or it can generate a state of confusion, which can easily turn to fear if we can't place the information into an understandable or meaningful organizational framework or context.

In our example, the child's sense of curiosity kicks in and he rushes to the dog to get more sensory experience. Notice how children are literally compelled to thrust themselves into a situation they know nothing about. However, in this example, the environmental forces at hand do not react favorably to the child's advances. The dog the child is interested in is either inherently mean or having a bad day. In any case, as soon as the child gets close enough, the dog bites him. The attack is so severe that the dog has to be pulled off the child.

This kind of unfortunate experience is certainly not typical, but it's not that uncommon either. I chose it for two reasons: First, most people can relate to it in some way, either from their own direct experience or through the experience of someone they know. Second, as we analyze the underlying dynamics of this experience from an energy perspective, we're going to learn about 1) how our minds are designed to think, 2) process information, 3) how these processes affect what we experience and 4) our ability to recognize new possibilities. I know this may seem like a lot of insight from just one example, but the principles involved apply to the dynamics beneath virtually all learning.

As a result of being physically and emotionally traumatized, the little boy in our example now has a memory and one distinction about the way dogs can express themselves. If the boy's ability to remember his experiences is normal, he can store this incident in a way that represents all of the senses the experience had an impact on: For example the attack can be stored as mental images based on what he saw, as well as mental sounds representing what he heard, and so on. Memories representing the other three senses will work the same way.

However, the kind of sensory data in his memory is not as important as the kind of energy the sensory data represents. We basically have two kinds of mental energy: positively charged energy, which we call love, confidence, happiness, joy, satisfaction, excitement, and enthusiasm, to name a few of the pleasant ways we can feel; and negatively charged energy, representing fear, terror, dissatisfaction, betrayal, regret, anger, confusion, anxiety, stress, and frustration, all representing what is commonly referred to as emotional pain.

Because the boy's first experience with a dog was intensely painful, we can assume that regardless of what senses were affected, all of his memories of this experience will be in painful, unpleasant-feeling, negative energy. Now, what effect will this negatively charged mental energy have on his perception and behavior if and when he encounters another dog? The answer is so obvious that it may seem ridiculous even to ask, but the underlying implications are not obvious, so bear with me. Clearly, the moment he comes into contact with another dog, he will experience fear.

Notice that I used the word "another" to describe the next dog he has any contact with. What I want to point out is that *any* dog can cause the boy to feel fear, not just the one that actually attacked him. It won't make a bit of difference if the next dog he comes into contact with is the friendliest dog in the world, one whose nature is only to express playfulness and love. The child will still be afraid, and furthermore, his fear could quickly turn to unrestrained terror especially if the second dog (seeing a child and wanting to play) attempts to approach him.

Each of us has at one time or another witnessed a situation in which someone was experiencing fear, when from our perspective there wasn't the least bit of danger or threat. Although we may not have said it, we probably thought to ourselves that this person was being irrational. If we tried to point out why there was no need to be afraid, we probably found that our words had little, if any, impact.

We could easily think the same thing about the boy in our example, that he is just being irrational, because it's clear from our perspective that other possibilities exist than the one his mind has focused on. But is his fear any less rational than, let's say, your fear (or hesitation) about putting on the next trade, when your last trade was a loser? Using the same logic, a top trader would say that your fear is irrational because this "now moment" opportunity has absolutely nothing to do with your last trade. Each trade is simply an edge with a probable outcome, and statistically independent of every other trade. If you believe otherwise, then I can see why you're afraid; but I can assure you that your fears are completely unfounded.

PERCEPTION AND RISK

As you can see, one person's perception of risk can easily be perceived as irrational thinking by another. Risk is relative, but to the person who perceives it in the moment, it seems absolute and beyond question. When the child encountered his first dog, he was bubbling with excitement and curiosity. What is it about the way our minds think and process information that could automatically flip the boy into a state of fear the next time he encounters a dog, even if it's months or years later? If we look at fear as a natural mechanism warning us of threatening conditions, then what is it about the way our minds function that would automatically tell the boy that the next encounter with a dog is something to be afraid of? What happened to the boy's natural sense of curiosity? There is surely more to learn about the nature of dogs than this one experience has taught him, especially in light of the fact that our minds seem to have an unlimited capacity for learning. And why would it be virtually impossible to talk the boy out of his fear?

THE POWER OF ASSOCIATION

As complex as these questions may seem at first glance, most of them can be answered quite easily. I'm sure many of you already know the answer: Our minds have an inherent design characteristic that causes us to associate and link anything that exists in the external environment that is similar in quality, characteristics, properties, or traits to anything that already exists in our mental environment as a memory or distinction. In other words, in the example of the child being afraid of dogs, the second dog or any other dog he encounters thereafter, doesn't have to be the dog that attacked in order for him to experience emotional pain. There just has to be enough of a likeness or similarity for his mind to make a connection between the two.

This natural tendency for our minds to associate is an unconscious mental function that occurs automatically. It's not something we have to think about or make a decision about. An unconscious mental function would be analogous to an involuntary physical function such as a heartbeat. Just as we don't have to consciously think about the process of making our hearts beat, we don't have to think about linking experiences and our feelings about them. It's simply a natural function of the way our minds process information, and, like a heartbeat, it's a function that has a profound effect on the way we experience our lives.

I'd like you to try and visualize the two-way flow of energy that reverses the cause-and-effect relationship that will make it difficult (if not impossible) for the boy to perceive any other possibilities than the one that's in his mind. To help you, I'm going to break this process down into its smallest parts, and go through what happens step by step. All of this may seem a bit abstract, but understanding this process plays a big part in unlocking your potential to achieve consistent success as a big trader.

First, let's get right down to the basics. There's structured energy on the outside of the boy and structured energy on the inside of the boy. The outside energy is positively charged in the form of a friendly dog that wants to express itself by playing. The inside energy is a negatively charged memory in the form of mental images and sounds that represent the boy's first experience with a dog.

Both the inside and the outside energy have the potential to make themselves felt on the boy's senses and, as a result, create two different kinds of situations for him to experience. The outside energy has the potential to act as a force on the boy in a way that he could find very enjoyable. This particular dog expresses behavior characteristics like playfulness, friendliness, and even love. But keep in mind that these are characteristics that the child still has not experienced in a dog, so from his perspective they don't exist. Just as in the price chart example I presented earlier, the child won't be able to perceive what he hasn't yet learned about, unless he is in a state of mind that is conducive to learning.

The inside energy also has potential and is just waiting, so to speak, to express itself. But it will act on the boy's eyes and ears in a way that causes him to feel threatened. This in turn will create an experience of emotional pain, fear, and possibly even terror.

From the way I've set this up, it may seem as if the boy has a choice between experiencing fun or experiencing fear, but that's really not the case, at least not in the moment. Of the two possibilities that exist in this situation, he will undoubtedly experience the pain and fear, instead of the fun. This is true for several reasons.

First, as I've already indicated, our minds are wired to automatically and instantaneously associate and link information that has similar characteristics, properties, and traits. What's outside of the child in the form of a dog, looks and sounds similar to the one that's in his mind. However, the degree of similarity that is necessary for his mind to link the two is an unknown variable, meaning I don't know the mental mechanism that determines how much or how little similarity is required for our minds to associate and link two or more sets of information. Since everyone's mind functions in a similar way, but, at the same time is unique, I would assume there is a range of tolerance for similarity or dissimilarity and each of us has a unique capacity somewhere within the range.

Here's what we do know: As this next dog comes into contact with the boy's eyes or ears, if there is enough similarity between the way it looks or sounds and the dog that's embedded in his memory, then his mind will automatically connect the two. This connection, in turn, will cause the negatively charged energy in his memory to be released throughout his body, causing him to be overcome with a very uncomfortable sense of foreboding or terror. The degree of discomfort or emotional pain that he experiences will be equivalent to the degree of trauma that he suffered as a result of his first encounter with a dog.

What happens next is what psychologists call a projection. I'm going to refer to it simply as another instantaneous association that makes the reality of the situation from the boy's perspective seem like the absolute, unquestionable truth. The boy's body is now filled with negatively charged energy. At the same time, he is in sensory contact with the dog. Next, his mind associates whatever sensory information his eyes or ears perceive with the painful energy he's experiencing inside himself, which makes it seem as if the source of his pain and fear is the dog he is seeing or hearing in that moment.

Psychologists call the dynamics of what I just described a projection because, in a sense, the boy is projecting the pain he is experiencing in the moment onto the dog. That painful energy then gets reflected back to him, so that he perceives a dog that is threatening, painful, and dangerous. This process makes the second dog identical in character, properties, and traits to the one that is in the boy's memory bank, even though the information the second dog is generating about its behavior is not identical, or even similar, to the behavior of the dog that actually attacked the boy.

Since the two dogs, the one in the boy's mind and the one outside of the boy's mind, feel exactly the same, it's extremely unlikely the boy will be able to make any type of distinctions in the second dog's behavior that would suggest to him that it is any different than the one in his mind. So, instead of perceiving this next encounter with a dog as an opportunity to experience something new about the nature of dogs, he perceives a threatening and dangerous dog.

Now, if you think about it for a moment, what is it about this process that would indicate to the boy that his experience of the situation was not the absolute, unquestionable truth? Certainly the pain and fear that he experienced in his body was the absolute truth.

But what about the possibilities that he perceived? Were they true? From our perspective, they weren't. However, from the boy's perspective, how could they be anything but the true reality of the situation? What alternatives did he have? First, he can't perceive possibilities that he hasn't learned about yet. And it is extremely difficult to learn anything new if you're afraid, because, as you already well know, fear is a very debilitating form of energy. It causes us to withdraw, to get ready to protect ourselves, to run, and to narrow our focus of attention—all of which makes it very difficult, if not impossible, to open ourselves in a way that allows us to learn something new.

Second, as I have already indicated, as far as the boy is concerned, the dog is the source of his pain, and in a sense this is true. The second dog did cause him to tap into the pain that was already in his mind, but it was not the true source of that pain. This was a positively charged dog that got connected to the boy's negatively charged energy by an automatic, involuntary mental process, functioning at speeds faster than it takes to blink an eye (a process that the boy has absolutely no awareness of). So as far as he's concerned, why would he be afraid if what he perceived about the dog wasn't the absolute truth?

As you can see, it wouldn't make any difference how the dog was acting, or what someone might say to the contrary about why the boy shouldn't be afraid, because he will perceive whatever information the dog is generating about itself (regardless of how positive) from a negative perspective. He will not have the slightest notion that his experience of pain, fear, and terror was completely self-generated.

Now, if it's possible for the boy to self-generate his own pain and terror and, at the same time, be firmly convinced that his negative experience was coming from the environment, is it also possible for traders to self-generate their own experiences of fear and emotional pain as they interact with market information and be thoroughly convinced that their pain and fear was completely justified by the circumstances? The underlining psychological dynamics work in exactly the same way.

One of your basic objectives as a trader is to perceive the opportunities available, not the threat of pain. To learn how to stay focused on the opportunities, you need to know and understand in no uncertain terms the source of the threat. It's not the market. The market generates information about its potential to move from a neutral perspective. At the same time, it provides you (the observer) with an unending stream of opportunities to do something on your own behalf. If what you perceive at any given moment causes you to feel fear, ask yourself this question: Is the information inherently threatening, or are you simply experiencing the effect of your own state of mind reflected back to you (as in the above illustration)?

I know this is a difficult concept to accept, so I'll give you another example to illustrate the point. Let's set up a scenario, where your last two or three trades were losers. You are watching the market, and the variables you use to indicate that an opportunity exists are now present. Instead of immediately executing the trade, you hesitate. The trade feels very risky, so risky, in fact, that you start questioning whether this is "really" a signal. As a result, you start gathering information to support why this trade probably won't work. This is information you normally wouldn't consider or pay attention to, and it's certainly not information that is part of your trading methodology.

In the meantime, the market is moving. Unfortunately, it is moving away from your original entry point, the point at which you would have gotten into the trade if you hadn't hesitated. Now you are conflicted, because you still want to get in; the thought of missing a winning trade is painful. At the same time, as the market moves away from your entry point, the dollar value of the risk to participate increases. The tug of war inside your mind intensifies. You don't want to miss out, but you don't want to get whipsawed either. In the end, you do nothing, because you are paralyzed by the conflict. You justify your state of immobility by telling yourself that it's just too risky to chase the market, while you agonize over every tic the market moves in the direction of what would have been a nice winning trade.

If this scenario sounds familiar, I want you to ask yourself whether, at the moment you hesitated, were you perceiving what the market was making available, or perceiving what was in your mind reflected back to you? The market gave you a signal. But you didn't perceive the signal from an objective or positive perspective. You didn't see it as an opportunity to experience the positive feeling you would get from winning or making money, but that's exactly what the market was making available to you.

Think about this for a moment: If I change the scenario so that your last two or three trades were winners instead of losers, would you have perceived the signal any differently? Would you have perceived it more as an opportunity to win than you did in the first scenario? If you were coming off three winners in a row, would you have hesitated to put that trade on? Very unlikely! In fact, if you're like most traders, you probably would have been giving very strong consideration to loading up (putting on a position much larger than your normal size).

In each situation, the market generated the same signal. But your state of mind was negative and fear-based in the first scenario, and that caused you to focus on the possibility of failure, which in turn caused you to hesitate. In the second scenario, you hardly perceived any risk at all. You may even have thought the market was making a dream come true. That, in turn, would make it easy, if not compelling, to financially overcommit yourself.

If you can accept the fact that the market doesn't generate positively or negatively charged information as an inherent characteristic of the way it expresses itself, then the only other way information can take on a positive or negative charge is in your mind, and that is a function of the way the information is processed. In other words, the market doesn't cause you to focus on failure and pain, or on winning and pleasure. What causes the information to take on a positive or negative quality is the same unconscious mental process that caused the boy to perceive the second dog as threatening and dangerous, when all the dog was offering was playfulness and friendship.

Our minds constantly associate what's outside of us (information) with something that's already in our mind (what we know), making it seem as if the outside circumstances and the memory, distinction, or belief these circumstances are associated with are exactly the same. As a result, in the first scenario, if you were coming off two or three losing trades, the next signal the market gives you that an opportunity was present will feel overly risky. Your mind is automatically and unconsciously linking the "now moment" with your most recent trading experiences. The link taps you into the pain of losing, creating a fearful state of mind and causing you to perceive the information you're exposed to in that moment from a negative perspective. It seems as if the market is expressing threatening information, so, of course, your hesitation is justified.

In the second scenario, the same process causes you to perceive the situation from an overly positive perspective, because you are coming off three winners in a row. The association between the "now moment" and the elation of the last three trades creates an overly positive or euphoric state of mind, making it seem as if the market is offering you a riskless opportunity. Of course, this justifies overcommitting yourself.

In Chapter 1, I said that many of the mental patterns that cause traders to lose and make errors are so self-evident and deeply ingrained that it would never occur to us that the reason we aren't consistently successful is because of the way we think. Understanding, becoming consciously aware of, and then learning how to circumvent the mind's natural propensity to associate is a big part of achieving that consistency. Developing and maintaining a state of mind that perceives the opportunity flow of the market, without the threat of pain or the problems caused by overconfidence, will require that you take conscious control of the association process.

CHAPTER 6

THE MARKET'S PERSPECTIVE

For the most part, a typical trader's perception of the risk in any given trading situation is a function of the outcome of his most recent two or three trades (depending on the individual). The best traders, on the other hand, are not impacted (either negatively or too positively) by the outcomes of their last or even their last several trades. So their perception of the risk of any given trading situation is not affected by this personal, psychological variable. There's a huge psychological gap here that might lead you to believe that the best traders have inherent design qualities in their minds that account for this gap, but I can assure you this is not the case.

Every trader I've worked with over the last 18 years has had to learn how to train his mind to stay properly focused in the "now moment opportunity flow." This is a universal problem, and has to do both with the way our minds are wired and our common social upbringing (meaning, this particular trading problem is not person-specific). There are other factors relating to self-esteem that may also act as obstacles to your consistent success, but what we are going to discuss now is the most important and fundamental building block to your success as a trader.

87

THE "UNCERTAINTY" PRINCIPLE

If there is such a thing as a secret to the nature of trading, this is it: At the very core of one's ability 1) to trade without fear or overconfidence, 2) perceive what the market is offering from its perspective, 3) stay completely focused in the "now moment opportunity flow," and 4) spontaneously enter the "zone," it is a strong virtually unshakeable belief in an uncertain outcome with an edge in your favor.

The best traders have evolved to the point where they believe, without a shred of doubt or internal conflict, that "anything can happen." They don't *just suspect* that anything can happen or give lip service to the idea. Their belief in uncertainty is so powerful that it actually prevents their minds from associating the "now moment" situation and circumstance with the outcomes of their most recent trades.

By preventing this association, they are able to keep their minds free of unrealistic and rigid expectations about how the market will express itself. Instead of generating the kind of unrealistic expectations that more often than not result in both emotional and financial pain, they have learned to "make themselves available" to take advantage of whatever opportunities the market may offer in any given moment.

"Making yourself available" is a perspective from which you understand that the framework from which you are perceiving information is limited relative to what's being offered. Our minds don't automatically perceive every opportunity that presents itself in any given moment. (The "boy and the dog" illustration from Chapter 5 is a perfect example of how our own personal versions of the truth are reflected back to us.)

This same kind of perceptual blindness happens all the time in trading. We can't perceive the potential for the market to continue to move in a direction that is already against our position if, for example, we are operating out of a fear of being wrong. The fear of admitting we are wrong causes us to place an inordinate amount of significance on information that tells us that we're right. This happens even if there's ample information to indicate that the market has in fact established a trend in the opposite direction of our position. A trending market is a distinction about the market's behavior we can ordinarily perceive, but this distinction can easily become invisible if we are operating out of fear. The trend and the opportunity to trade in the direction of that trend don't become visible until we are out of the trade.

In addition, there are opportunities that are invisible to us because we haven't learned to make the distinctions that would allow us to perceive them. Recall our discussion in Chapter 5 of the first price chart you ever looked at. What we haven't learned yet is invisible to us, and remains invisible until our minds are open to an exchange of energy.

A perspective from which you make yourself available takes into consideration both the known and the unknown: For example, you've built a mental framework that allows you to recognize a set of variables in the market's behavior that indicates when an opportunity to buy or sell is present. This is your edge and something you know. However, what you don't know is exactly how the pattern your variables identify will unfold.

With the perspective of making yourself available, you know that your edge places the odds of success in your favor, but, at the same time, you completely accept the fact that you don't know the outcome of any particular trade. By making yourself available, you consciously open yourself up to find out what will happen next; instead of giving way to an automatic mental process that causes you to think you already know. Adopting this perspective leaves your mind free of internal resistance that can prevent you from perceiving whatever opportunity the market is making available from its perspective (its truth). Your mind is open for an exchange of energy. Not only can you learn something about the market that you previously didn't know, but you also set up the mental condition most conducive to entering "the zone."

The essence of what it means to be in "the zone" is that your mind and the market are in sync. As a result, you sense what the market is about to do as if there is no separation between yourself and the collective consciousness of everyone else participating in the market. The zone is a mental space where you are doing more than just reading the collective mind, you are also in complete harmony with it.

If this sounds a bit strange to you, ask yourself how it is that a flock of birds or a school of fish can change direction simultaneously. There must be a way in which they are linked to one another. If it is possible for people to become linked in the same way, then there will be times when information from those with whom we are linked can and will bleed through to our consciousness. Traders who have experienced being tapped into the collective consciousness of the market can anticipate a change in direction just as a bird in the middle of a flock or a fish in the middle of a school will turn at the precise moment that all of the others turn.

However, setting up the kind of mental conditions most conducive to experiencing this seemingly magical synchronicity between you and the market is no easy task. There are two mental hurdles to overcome. The first is the focus of this chapter: learning how to keep your mind focused in the "now moment opportunity flow." In order to experience synchronicity, your mind has to be open to the market's truth, from its perspective.

The second hurdle has to do with the division of labor between the two halves of our brain. The left side of our brain specializes in rational thought, based on what we already know. The right side specializes in creative thought. It is capable of tapping into an inspiration, an intuition, a hunch, or a sense of knowing that usually can't be explained at a rational level. It can't be explained because if the information is really creative in nature, then it is something that we wouldn't know at a rational level. By definition, true creativity brings forth something that didn't previously exist. There's an inherent conflict between these two modes of thought, that the rational, logical part will almost always win, unless we take specific steps to train our minds to accept and trust creative information. Without that training, we will usually find it very difficult to act on our hunches, intuitive impulses, inspirations, or sense of knowing.

Acting appropriately on anything requires belief and clarity of intent, which keeps our minds and senses focused on the purpose at hand. If the source of our actions is creative in nature, and our rational mind hasn't been properly trained to trust this source, then at some point in the process of acting on this information, our rational brain will flood our consciousness with conflicting and competing thoughts. Of course, all of these thoughts will be sound and reasonable in nature, because they will be coming from what we already know at a rational level, but they will have the effect of flipping us out of "the zone" or any other creative state of mind. There are few things in life more frustrating than recognizing the possibilities evident from a hunch, intuition, or an inspired idea, and not taking advantage of that potential because we talked ourselves out of it.

I realize that what I've just said is still much too abstract to implement on a practical basis. So, I'm going to take you step-by-step through what it means to be completely focused in the "now moment opportunity flow." My objective is that by the time you've read this chapter and Chapter 7, you will understand without a shred of doubt why your ultimate success as a trader cannot be realized until you develop a resolute, unshakeable belief in uncertainty.

The first step on the road toward getting your mind and the market in sync is to understand and completely accept the psychological realities of trading. This step is where most of the frustrations, disappointments, and mysteriousness associated with trading begin. Very few people who decide to trade ever take the time or expend the effort to think about what it means to be a trader. Most people who go into trading think that being a trader is synonymous with being a good market analyst.

As I have mentioned, this couldn't be further from the truth. Good market analysis can certainly contribute to and play a supporting role in one's success, but it doesn't deserve the attention and importance most traders mistakenly attach to it. Beneath the market behavior patterns that are so easy to become fixated on are some very unique psychological characteristics. It's the nature of these psychological characteristics that determines how one needs "to be" in order to operate effectively in the market environment.

Operating effectively in an environment that has qualities, traits, or characteristics that are different from what we're used to requires making some adjustments or changes in the way we normally think about things. For example, if you were to travel to an exotic place with certain objectives or goals to accomplish, the first thing you would do is familiarize yourself with the local traditions and customs. By doing so, you would learn about the various ways in which you would have to adapt in order to function successfully in that environment.

Traders frequently ignore the fact that they may have to adapt in order to become consistently successful traders. There are two reasons for this. The first is that you need absolutely no skill of any kind to put on a winning trade. For most traders it usually takes years of pain and suffering before they figure out or finally admit to themselves that there's more to being consistent than the ability to pick an occasional winner.

The second reason is that you don't have to travel anywhere to trade. All you need is access to a phone. You don't even have to roll out of bed in the morning. Even traders who normally trade from an office don't have to be in the office to put on or take off their trades. Because we can access and interact with the market from personal environments that we are intimately familiar with, it seems as if trading won't require any special adaptations in the way we think.

To some degree, you are probably already aware of many of the fundamental truths (psychological characteristics) about the nature of trading. But having an awareness or an understanding of some principle, insight, or concept doesn't necessarily equate to acceptance and belief. When something has been truly accepted, it isn't in conflict with any other component of our mental environment. When we believe in something, we operate out of that belief as a natural function of who we are, without struggle or extra effort. To whatever degree there is a conflict with any other component of our mental environment, to the same degree there is a lack of acceptance.

It isn't difficult, therefore, to understand why so few people make it as traders. They simply don't do the mental work necessary to reconcile the many conflicts that exist between what they've already learned and believe, and how that learning contradicts and acts as a source of resistance to implementing the various principles of successful trading. Getting into and taking advantage of the kind of free-flowing states of mind that are ideal for trading requires that those conflicts be thoroughly resolved.

THE MARKET'S MOST FUNDAMENTAL CHARACTERISTIC
(IT CAN EXPRESS ITSELF IN AN ALMOST INFINITE COMBINATION OF WAYS)

The market can do virtually anything at any time. This seems obvious enough, especially for anybody who has experienced a market that has displayed erratic and volatile price swings. The problem is that all of us have the tendency to take this characteristic for granted, in ways that cause us to make the most fundamental trading errors over and over again. The fact is that if traders really believed that anything could happen at any time, there would be considerably fewer losers and more consistent winners.

How do we know that virtually anything can happen? This fact is easy to establish. All we have to do is dissect the market into its component parts and look at how the parts operate. The most fundamental component of any market is its traders. Individual traders act as a force on prices, making them move by either bidding a price up or offering it lower.

Why do traders bid a price up or offer it lower? To answer this question we have to establish the reasons why people trade. There are many reasons and purposes behind a person's motivation to trade in any given market. However, for the purposes of this illustration, we don't have to know all the underlying reasons that compel any individual trader to act because ultimately they all boil down to one reason and one purpose: to make money. We know this because there are only two things a trader can do (buy and sell) and there are only two possible outcomes for every trade (profit or loss).

Therefore, I think we can safely assume that regardless of one's reasons for trading, the bottom line is that everyone is looking for the same outcome: Profits. And there are only two ways to create those profits: Either buy low and sell high, or sell high and buy low. If we assume that everyone wants to make money, then there's only one reason why any trader would bid a price up to the next highest level: because he believes he can sell whatever he's buying at a higher price at some point in the future. The same is true for the trader who's willing to sell something at a price that is less than the last posted price (offer a market lower). He does it because he believes he can buy back whatever he's selling at a lower price at some point in the future.

If we look at the market's behavior as a function of price movement, and if price movement is a function of traders who are willing to bid prices up or offer them lower, then we can say that all price movement (market behavior) is a function of what traders believe about the future. To be more specific, all price movement is a function of what individual traders believe about what is high and what is low.

The underlying dynamics of market behavior are quite simple. Only three primary forces exist in any market: traders who believe the price is low, traders who believe the price is high, and traders who are watching and waiting to make up their minds about whether the price is low or high. Technically, the third group constitutes a potential force. The reasons that support any given trader's belief that something is high or low are usually irrelevant, because most people who trade act in an undisciplined, unorganized, haphazard, and random manner. So, their reasons wouldn't necessarily help anyone gain a better understanding of what is going on.

But, understanding what's going on isn't that difficult, if you remember that all price movement or lack of movement is a function of the relative balance or imbalance between two primary forces: traders who believe the price is going up, and traders who believe the price is going down. If there's balance between the two groups, prices will stagnate, because each side will absorb the force of the other side's actions. If there is an imbalance, prices will move in the direction of the greater force, or the traders who have the stronger convictions in their beliefs about in what direction the price is going.

Now, I want you to ask yourself, what's going to stop virtually anything from happening at any time, other than exchange-imposed limits on price movement. There's nothing to stop the price of an issue from going as high or low as whatever some trader in the world believes is possible—if, of course, the trader is willing to act on that belief. So the range of the market's behavior in its collective form is limited only by the most extreme beliefs about what is high and what is low held by any given individual participating in that market. I think the implications are self-evident: There can be an extreme diversity of beliefs present in any given market in any given moment, making virtually anything possible.

When we look at the market from this perspective, it's easy to see that every potential trader who is willing to express his belief about the future becomes a market variable. On a more personal level, this means that it only takes one other trader, anywhere in the world, to negate the positive potential of your trade. Put another way, it takes only one other trader to negate what you believe about what is high or what is low. That's all, only one!

Here's an example to illustrate this point. Several years ago, a trader came to me for help. He was an excellent market analyst; in fact, he was one of the best I've ever met. But after years of frustration during which he lost all his money and a lot of other people's money, he was finally ready to admit that, as a trader, he left a lot to be desired. After talking to him for a while, I determined that a number of serious psychological obstacles were preventing him from being successful. One of the most troublesome obstacles was that he was a know-it-all and extremely arrogant, making it impossible for him to achieve the degree of mental flexibility required to trade effectively. It didn't matter how good an analyst he was. When he came to me, he was so desperate for money and help that he was willing to consider anything.

The first suggestion I made was that instead of looking for another investor to back what ultimately would be another failed attempt at trading, he would be better off taking a job, doing something he was truly good at. He could be paid a steady income while working through his problems, and at the same time provide someone with a worthwhile service. He took my advice and quickly found a position as a technical analyst with a fairly substantial brokerage house and clearing firm in Chicago.

The semiretired chairman of the board of the brokerage firm was a longtime trader with nearly 40 years of experience in the grain pits at the Chicago Board of Trade. He didn't know much about technical analysis, because he never needed it to make money on the floor. But he no longer traded on the floor and found the transition to trading from a screen difficult and somewhat mysterious. So he asked the firm's newly acquired star technical analyst to sit with him during the trading day and teach him technical trading. The new hire jumped at the opportunity to show off his abilities to such an experienced and successful trader.

The analyst was using a method called "point and line," developed by Charlie Drummond. (Among other things, point and line can accurately define support and resistance.) One day, as the two of them were watching the soybean market together, the analyst had projected major support and resistance points and the market happened to be trading between these two points. As the technical analyst was explaining to the chairman the significance of these two points, he stated in very emphatic, almost absolute terms that if the market goes up to resistance, it will stop and reverse; and if the market goes down to support, it will also stop and reverse. Then he explained that if the market went down to the price level he calculated as support, his calculations indicated that would also be the low of the day.

As they sat there, the bean market was slowly trending down to the price the analyst said would be the support, or low, of the day. When it finally got there, the chairman looked over to the analyst and said, "This is where the market is supposed to stop and go higher, right?" The analyst responded, "Absolutely! This is the low of the day." "That's bullshit!" the chairman retorted. "Watch this." He picked up the phone, called one of the clerks handling orders for the soybean pit, and said, "Sell two million beans (bushels) at the market." Within thirty seconds after he placed the order, the soybean market dropped ten cents a bushel. The chairman turned to look at the horrified expression on the analyst's face. Calmly, he asked, "Now, where did you say the market was going to stop? If I can do that, anyone can."

The point is that from our own individual perspective as observers of the market, anything can happen, and it takes only one trader to do it. This is the hard, cold reality of trading that only the very best traders have embraced and accepted with no internal conflict. How do I know this? Because only the best traders consistently predefine their risks before entering a trade. Only the best traders cut their losses without reservation or hesitation when the market tells them the trade isn't working. And only the best traders have an organized, systematic, money-management regimen for taking profits when the market goes in the direction of their trade.

Not predefining your risk, not cutting your losses, or not systematically taking profits are three of the most common—and usually the most costly—trading errors you can make. Only the best traders have eliminated these errors from their trading. At some point in their careers, they learned to believe without a shred of doubt that anything can happen, and to **always** account for what they don't know, for the unexpected.

Remember that there are only two forces that cause prices to move: traders who believe the markets are going up, and traders who believe the markets are going down. At any given moment, we can see who has the stronger conviction by observing where the market is now relative to where it was at some previous moment. If a recognizable pattern is present, that pattern may repeat itself, giving us an indication of where the market is headed. This is our edge, something we know.

But there's also much that we don't know, and will never know unless we learn how to read minds. For instance, do we know how many traders may be sitting on the sidelines and about to enter the market? Do we know how many of them want to buy and how many want to sell, or how many shares they are willing to buy or sell? What about the traders whose participation is already reflected in the current price? At any given moment, how many of them are about to change their minds and exit their positions? If they do, how long will they stay out of the market? And if and when they do come back into the market, in what direction will they cast their votes?

These are the constant, never-ending, unknown, hidden variables that are always operating in every market—*always*! The best traders don't try to hide from these unknown variables by pretending they don't exist, nor do they try to intellectualize or rationalize them away through market analysis. Quite the contrary, the best traders take these variables into account, factoring them into every component of their trading regimes.

For the typical trader, just the opposite is true. He trades from the perspective that what he can't see, hear, or feel must not exist. What other explanation could account for his behavior? If he really believed in the existence of all the hidden variables that have the potential to act on prices in any given moment, then he would also have to believe that every trade has an uncertain outcome. And if every trade truly has an uncertain outcome, then how could he ever justify or talk himself into not predefining his risk, cutting his losses, or having some systematic way to take profits? Given the circumstances, not adhering to these three fundamental principles is the equivalent of committing financial and emotional suicide.

Since most traders don't adhere to these principles, are we to assume that their true underlying motivation for trading is to destroy themselves? It's certainly possible, but I think the percentage of traders who either consciously or subconsciously want to rid themselves of their money or hurt themselves in some way is extremely small. So, if financial suicide is not the predominant reason, then what could keep someone from doing something that would otherwise make absolute, perfect sense? The answer is quite simple: The typical trader doesn't predefine his risk, cut his losses, or systematically take profits because the typical trader doesn't believe it's necessary. The only reason why he would believe it isn't necessary is that he believes he already knows what's going to happen next, based on what he perceives is happening in any given "now moment." If he already knows, then there's really no reason to adhere to these principles. Believing, assuming, or thinking that "he knows" will be the cause of virtually every trading error he has the potential to make (with the exception of those errors that are the result of not believing that he deserves the money).

Our beliefs about what is true and real are very powerful inner forces. They control every aspect of how we interact with the markets, from our perceptions, interpretations, decisions, actions, and expectations, to our feelings about the results. It's extremely difficult to act in a way that contradicts what we believe to be true. In some cases, depending on the strength of the belief, it can be next to impossible to do anything that violates the integrity of a belief.

What the typical trader doesn't realize is that he needs an inner mechanism, in the form of some powerful beliefs, that virtually compels him to perceive the market from a perspective that is always expanding with greater and greater degrees of clarity, and also compels him always act appropriately, given the psychological conditions and the nature of price movement. The most effective and functional trading belief that he can acquire is "anything can happen." Aside from the fact that it is the truth, it will act as a solid foundation for building every other belief and attitude that he needs to be a successful trader.

Without that belief, his mind will automatically, and usually without his conscious awareness, cause him to avoid, block, or rationalize away any information that indicates the market may do something he hasn't accepted as possible. If he believes that anything is possible, then there's nothing for his mind to avoid. Because *anything* includes everything, this belief will act as an expansive force on his perception of the market that will allow him to perceive information that might otherwise have been invisible to him. In essence, he will be making himself available (opening his mind) to perceive more of the possibilities that exist from the market's perspective.

Most important, by establishing a belief that anything can happen, he will be training his mind to think in probabilities. This is by far the most essential as well as the most difficult principle for people to grasp and to effectively integrate into their mental systems.

CHAPTER 7

THE TRADER'S EDGE:
THINKING IN
PROBABILITIES

Exactly what does it mean to think in probabilities, and why is it so essential to one's consistent success as a trader? If you take a moment and analyze the last sentence, you will notice that I made consistency a function of probabilities. It sounds like a contradiction: How can someone produce consistent results from an event that has an uncertain probabilistic outcome? To answer this question, all we have to do is look to the gambling industry.

Corporations spend vast amounts of money, in the hundreds of millions, if not billions, of dollars, on elaborate hotels to attract people to their casinos. If you've been to Las Vegas you know exactly what I am talking about. Gaming corporations are just like other corporations, in that they have to justify how they allocate their assets to a board of directors and ultimately to their stockholders. How do you suppose they justify spending vast sums of money on elaborate hotels and casinos, whose primary function is to generate revenue from an event that has a purely random outcome?

PARADOX: RANDOM OUTCOME, CONSISTENT RESULTS

Here's an interesting paradox. Casinos make consistent profits day after day and year after year, facilitating an event that has a purely random outcome. At the same time, most traders believe that the outcome of the market's behavior is not random, yet can't seem to produce consistent profits. Shouldn't a consistent, nonrandom outcome produce consistent results, and a random outcome produce random, inconsistent results?

What casino owners, experienced gamblers, and the best traders understand that the typical trader finds difficult to grasp is: Events that have probable outcomes can produce consistent results, if you can get the odds in your favor and there is a large enough sample size. The best traders treat trading like a numbers game, similar to the way in which casinos and professional gamblers approach gambling.

To illustrate, let's look at the game of blackjack. In blackjack, the casinos have approximately a 4.5-percent edge over the player, based on the rules they require players to adhere to. This means that, over a large enough sample size (number of hands played), the casino will generate net profits of four and a half cents on every dollar wagered on the game. This average of four and a half cents takes into account all the players who walked away big winners (including all winning streaks), all the players who walked away big losers, and everybody in between. At the end of the day, week, month, or year, the casino always ends up with approximately 4.5 percent of the total amount wagered.

That 4.5 percent might not sound like a lot, but let's put it in perspective. Suppose a total of $100 million dollars is wagered collectively at all of a casino's blackjack tables over the course of a year. The casino will net $4.5 million.

What casino owners and professional gamblers understand about the nature of probabilities is that each individual hand played is statistically independent of every other hand. This means that each individual hand is a unique event, where the outcome is random relative to the last hand played or the next hand played. If you focus on each hand individually, there will be a random, unpredictable distribution between winning and losing hands. But on a collective basis, just the opposite is true. If a large enough number of hands is played, patterns will emerge that produce a consistent, predictable, and statistically reliable outcome.

Here's what makes thinking in probabilities so difficult. It requires two layers of beliefs that on the surface seem to contradict each other. We'll call the first layer the micro level. At this level, you have to believe in the uncertainty and unpredictability of the outcome of each individual hand. You know the truth of this uncertainty, because there are always a number of unknown variables affecting the consistency of the deck that each new hand is drawn from. For example, you can't know in advance how any of the other participants will decide to play their hands, since they can either take or decline additional cards. Any variables acting on the consistency of the deck that can't be controlled or known in advance will make the outcome of any particular hand both uncertain and random (statistically independent) in relationship to any other hand.

The second layer is the macro level. At this level, you have to believe that the outcome over a series of hands played is relatively certain and predictable. The degree of certainty is based on the fixed or constant variables that are known in advance and specifically designed to give an advantage (edge) to one side or the other. The constant variables I am referring to are the rules of the game. So, even though you don't or couldn't know in advance (unless you are psychic) the sequence of wins to losses, you can be relatively certain that if enough hands are played, whoever has the edge will end up with more wins than losses. The degree of certainty is a function of how good the edge is.

It's the ability to believe in the unpredictability of the game at the micro level and simultaneously believe in the predictability of the game at the macro level that makes the casino and the professional gambler effective and successful at what they do. Their belief in the uniqueness of each hand prevents them from engaging in the pointless endeavor of trying to predict the outcome of each individual hand. They have learned and completely accepted the fact that they don't know what's going to happen next. More important, they don't need to know in order to make money consistently.

Because they don't have to know what's going to happen next, they don't place any special significance, emotional or otherwise, on each individual hand, spin of the wheel, or roll of the dice. In other words, they're not encumbered by unrealistic expectations about what is going to happen, nor are their egos involved in a way that makes them have to be right. As a result, it's easier to stay focused on keeping the odds in their favor and executing flawlessly, which in turn makes them less susceptible to making costly mistakes. They stay relaxed because they are committed and willing to let the probabilities (their edges) play themselves out, all the while knowing that if their edges are good enough and the sample sizes are big enough, they will come out net winners.

The best traders use the same thinking strategy as the casino and professional gambler. Not only does it work to their benefit, but the underlying dynamics supporting the need for such a strategy are exactly the same in trading as they are in gambling. A simple comparison between the two will demonstrate this quite clearly.

First, the trader, the gambler, and the casino are all dealing with both known and unknown variables that affect the outcome of each trade or gambling event. In gambling, the known variables are the rules of the game. In trading, the known variables (from each individual trader's perspective) are the results of their market analysis.

Market analysis finds behavior patterns in the collective actions of everyone participating in a market. We know that individuals will act the same way under similar situations and circumstances, over and over again, producing observable patterns of behavior. By the same token, groups of individuals interacting with one another, day after day, week after week, also produce behavior patterns that repeat themselves.

These collective behavior patterns can be discovered and subsequently identified by using analytical tools such as trend lines, moving averages, oscillators, or retracements, just to name a few of the thousands that are available to any trader. Each analytical tool uses a set of criteria to define the boundaries of each behavior pattern identified. The set of criteria and the boundaries identified are the trader's known market variables. They are to the individual trader what the rules of the game are to the casino and gambler. By this I mean, the trader's analytical tools are the known variables that put the odds of success (the edge) for any given trade in the trader's favor, in the same way that the rules of the game put the odds of success in favor of the casino.

Second, we know that in gambling a number of unknown variables act on the outcome of each game. In blackjack, the unknowns are the shuffling of the deck and how the players choose to play their hands. In craps, it's how the dice are thrown. And in roulette, it's the amount of force applied to spin the wheel. All these unknown variables act as forces on the outcome of each individual event, in a way that causes each event to be statistically independent of any other individual event, thereby creating a random distribution between wins and losses.

Trading also involves a number of unknown variables that act on the outcome of any particular behavior pattern a trader may identify and use as his edge. In trading, the unknown variables are all other traders who have the potential to come into the market to put on or take off a trade. Each trade contributes to the market's position at any given moment, which means that each trader, acting on a belief about what is high and what is low, contributes to the collective behavior pattern that is displayed at that moment.

If there is a recognizable pattern, and if the variables used to define that pattern conform to a particular trader's definition of an edge, then we can say that the market is offering the trader an opportunity to buy low or sell high, based on the trader's definition. Suppose the trader seizes the opportunity to take advantage of his edge and puts on a trade. What factors will determine whether the market unfolds in the direction of his edge or against it? The answer is: the behavior of other traders!

At the moment he puts a trade on, and for as long as he chooses to stay in that trade, other traders will be participating in that market. They will be acting on their beliefs about what is high and what is low. At any given moment, some percentage of other traders will contribute to an outcome favorable to our trader's edge, and the participation of some percentage of traders will negate his edge. There's no way to know in advance how everyone else is going to behave and how their behavior will affect his trade, so the outcome of the trade is uncertain. The fact is, the outcome of every (legal) trade that anyone decides to make is affected in some way by the subsequent behavior of other traders participating in that market, making the outcome of all trades uncertain.

Since all trades have an uncertain outcome, then like gambling, each trade has to be statistically independent of the next trade, the last trade, or any trades in the future, even though the trader may use the same set of known variables to identify his edge for each trade. Furthermore, if the outcome of each individual trade is statistically independent of every other trade, there must also be a random distribution between wins and losses in any given string or set of trades, even though the odds of success for each individual trade may be in the trader's favor.

Third, casino owners don't try to predict or know in advance the outcome of each individual event. Aside from the fact that it would be extremely difficult, given all the unknown variables operating in each game, it isn't necessary to create consistent results. Casino operators have learned that all they have to do is keep the odds in their favor and have a large enough sample size of events so that their edges have ample opportunity to work.

TRADING IN THE MOMENT

Traders who have learned to think in probabilities approach the markets from virtually the same perspective. At the micro level, they believe that each trade or edge is unique. What they understand about the nature of trading is that at any given moment, the market may look exactly the same on a chart as it did at some previous moment; and the geometric measurements and mathematical calculations used to determine each edge can be exactly the same from one edge to the next; but the actual consistency of the market itself from one moment to the next is never the same.

For any particular pattern to be exactly the same now as it was in some previous moment would require that every trader who participated in that previous moment be present. What's more, each of them would also have to interact with one another in exactly the same way over some period of time to produce the exact same outcome to whatever pattern was being observed. The odds of that happening are nonexistent.

It is extremely important that you understand this phenomenon because the psychological implications for your trading couldn't be more important. We can use all the various tools to analyze the market's behavior and find the patterns that represent the best edges, and from an analytical perspective, these patterns can appear to be precisely the same in every respect, both mathematically and visually. But, if the consistency of the group of traders who are creating the pattern "now" is different by even one person from the group that created the pattern in the past, then the outcome of the current pattern has the potential to be different from the past pattern. (The example of the analyst and chairman illustrates this point quite well.) It takes only one trader, somewhere in the world, with a different belief about the future to change the outcome of any particular market pattern and negate the edge that pattern represents.

The most fundamental characteristic of the market's behavior is that each "now moment" market situation, each "now moment" behavior pattern, and each "now moment" edge is always a unique occurrence with its own outcome, independent of all others. Uniqueness implies that anything can happen, either what we know (expect or anticipate), or what we don't know (or can't know, unless we had extraordinary perceptual abilities). A constant flow of both known and unknown variables creates a probabilistic environment where we don't know for certain what will happen next.

This last statement may seem quite logical, even self-evident, but there's a huge problem here that is anything but logical or self-evident. Being aware of uncertainty and understanding the nature of probabilities does not equate with an ability to actually function effectively from a probabilistic perspective. Thinking in probabilities can be difficult to master, because our minds don't naturally process information in this manner. Quite the contrary, our minds cause us to perceive what we know, and what we know is part of our past, whereas, in the market, every moment is new and unique, even though there may be similarities to something that occurred in the past.

This means that unless we train our minds to perceive the uniqueness of each moment, that uniqueness will automatically be filtered out of our perception. We will perceive only what we know, minus any information that is blocked by our fears; everything else will remain invisible. The bottom line is that there is some degree of sophistication to thinking in probabilities, which can take some people a considerable amount of effort to integrate into their mental systems as a functional thinking strategy. Most traders don't fully understand this; as a result, they mistakenly assume they are thinking in probabilities, because they have some degree of understanding of the concepts.

I've worked with hundreds of traders who mistakenly assumed they thought in probabilities, but didn't. Here is an example of a trader I worked with whom I'll call Bob. Bob is a certified trading advisor (CTA) who manages approximately $50 million in investments. He's been in the business for almost 30 years. He came to one of my workshops because he was never able to produce more than a 12- to 18-percent annual return on the accounts he managed. This was an adequate return, but Bob was extremely dissatisfied because his analytical abilities suggested that he should be achieving an annual return of 150 to 200 percent.

I would describe Bob as being well-versed in the nature of probabilities. In other words, he understood the concepts, but he didn't function from a probabilistic perspective. Shortly after attending the workshop, he called to ask me for some advice. Here is the entry from my journal written immediately after that phone conversation.

9-28-95: Bob called with a problem. He put on a belly trade and put his stop in the market. The market traded about a third of the way to his stop and then went back to his entry point, where he decided to bail out of the trade. Almost immediately after he got out, the bellies went 500 points in the direction of this trade, but of course he was out of the market. He didn't understand what was going on.

First, I asked him what was at risk. He didn't understand the question. He assumed that he had accepted the risk because he put in a stop. I responded that just because he put in a stop it didn't mean that he had truly accepted the risk of the trade. There are many things that can be at risk: losing money, being wrong, not being perfect, etc., depending on one's underlying motivation for trading. I pointed out that a person's beliefs are always revealed by their actions. We can assume that he was operating out of a belief that to be a disciplined trader one has to define the risk and put a stop in. And so he did. But a person can put in a stop and at the same time not believe that he is going to be stopped out or that the trade will ever work against him, for that matter.

By the way he described the situation, it sounded to me as if this is exactly what happened to him. When he put on the trade, he didn't believe he would be stopped out. Nor did he believe the market would trade against him. In fact, he was so adamant about this, that when the market came back to his entry point, he got out of the trade to punish the market with an "I'll show you" attitude for even going against him by one tic.

After I pointed this out to him, he said this was exactly the attitude he had when he took off the trade. He said that he had been waiting for this particular trade for weeks and when the market finally got to this point, he thought it would immediately reverse. I responded by reminding him to look at the experience as simply pointing the way to something that he needs to learn. A prerequisite for thinking in probabilities is that you accept the risk, because if you don't, you will not want to face the possibilities that you haven't accepted, if and when they do present themselves.

When you've trained your mind to think in probabilities, it means you have fully accepted all the possibilities (with no internal resistance or conflict) and you always do something to take the unknown forces into account. Thinking this way is virtually impossible unless you've done the mental work necessary to "let go" of the need to know what is going to happen next or the need to be right on each trade. In fact, the degree by which you think you know, assume you know, or in any way need to know what is going to happen next, is equal to the degree to which you will fail as a trader.

Traders who have learned to think in probabilities are confident of their overall success, because they commit themselves to taking every trade that conforms to their definition of an edge. They don't attempt to pick and choose the edges they think, assume, or believe are going to work and act on those; nor do they avoid the edges that for whatever reason they think, assume, or believe aren't going to work. If they did either of those things, they would be contradicting their belief that the "now" moment situation is always unique, creating a random distribution between wins and losses on any given string of edges. They have learned, usually quite painfully, that they don't know in advance which edges are going to work and which ones aren't. They have stopped trying to predict outcomes. They have found that by taking every edge, they correspondingly increase their sample size of trades, which in turn gives whatever edge they use ample opportunity to play itself out in their favor, just like the casinos.

On the other hand, why do you think unsuccessful traders are obsessed with market analysis. They crave the sense of certainty that analysis appears to give them. Although few would admit it, the truth is that the typical trader wants to be right on every single trade. He is desperately trying to create certainty where it just doesn't exist. The irony is that if he completely accepted the fact that certainty doesn't exist, he would create the certainty he craves: He would be absolutely certain that certainty doesn't exist.

When you achieve complete acceptance of the uncertainty of each edge and the uniqueness of each moment, your frustration with trading will end. Furthermore, you will no longer be susceptible to making all the typical trading errors that detract from your potential to be consistent and destroy your sense of self-confidence. For example, not defining the risk before getting into a trade is by far the most common of all trading errors, and starts the whole process of trading from an inappropriate perspective. In light of the fact that anything can happen, wouldn't it make perfect sense to decide before executing a trade what the market has to look, sound, or feel like to tell you your edge isn't working? So why doesn't the typical trader decide to do it or do it every single time?

I have already given you the answer in the last chapter, but there's more to it and there's also some tricky logic involved, but the answer is simple. The typical trader won't predefine the risk of getting into a trade because he doesn't believe it's necessary. The only way he could believe "it isn't necessary" is if he believes he knows what's going to happen next. The reason he believes he knows what's going to happen next is because he won't get into a trade until he is convinced that he's right. At the point where he's convinced the trade will be a winner, it's no longer necessary to define the risk (because if he's right, there is no risk).

Typical traders go through the exercise of convincing themselves that they're right before they get into a trade, because the alternative (being wrong) is simply unacceptable. Remember that our minds are wired to associate. As a result, being wrong on any given trade has the potential to be associated with any (or every) other experience in a trader's life where he's been wrong. The implication is that any trade can easily tap him into the accumulated pain of every time he has been wrong in his life. Given the huge backlog of unresolved, negative energy surrounding what it means to be wrong that exists in most people, it's easy to see why each and every trade can literally take on the significance of a life or death situation.

So, for the typical trader, determining what the market would have to look, sound, or feel like to tell him that a trade isn't working would create an irreconcilable dilemma. On one hand, he desperately wants to win and the only way he can do that is to participate, but the only way he will participate is if he's sure the trade will win.

On the other hand, if he defines his risk, he is willfully gathering evidence that would negate something he has already convinced himself of. He will be contradicting the decision-making process he went through to convince himself that the trade will work. If he exposed himself to conflicting information, it would surely create some degree of doubt about the viability of the trade. If he allows himself to experience doubt, it's very unlikely he will participate. If he doesn't put the trade on and it turns out to be a winner, he will be in extreme agony. For some people, nothing hurts more than an opportunity recognized but missed because of self-doubt. For the typical trader, the only way out of this psychological dilemma is to ignore the risk and remain convinced that the trade is right.

If any of this sounds familiar, consider this: When you're convincing yourself that you're right, what you're saying to yourself is, "I know who's in this market and who's about to come into this market. I know what they believe about what is high or what is low. Furthermore, I know each individual's capacity to act on those beliefs (the degree of clarity or relative lack of inner conflict), and with this knowledge, I am able to determine how the actions of each of these individuals will affect price movement in its collective form a second, a minute, an hour, a day, or a week from now." Looking at the process of convincing yourself that you're right from this perspective, it seems a bit absurd, doesn't it?

For the traders who have learned to think in probabilities, there is no dilemma. Predefining the risk doesn't pose a problem for these traders because they don't trade from a right or wrong perspective. They have learned that trading doesn't have anything to do with being right or wrong on any individual trade. As a result, they don't perceive the risks of trading in the same way the typical trader does.

Any of the best traders (the probability thinkers) could have just as much negative energy surrounding what it means to be wrong as the typical trader. But as long as they legitimately define trading as a probability game, their emotional responses to the outcome of any particular trade are equivalent to how the typical trader would feel about flipping a coin, calling heads, and seeing the coin come up tails. A wrong call, but for most people being wrong about predicting the flip of a coin *would not* tap them into the accumulated pain of every other time in their lives they had been wrong.

Why? Most people know that the outcome of a coin toss is random. If you believe the outcome is random, then you naturally expect a random outcome. Randomness implies at least some degree of uncertainty. So when we believe in a random outcome, there is an implied acceptance that we don't know what that outcome will be. When we accept in advance of an event that we don't know how it will turn out, that acceptance has the effect of keeping our expectations neutral and open-ended.

Now we're getting down to the very core of what ails the typical trader. Any expectation about the market's behavior that is specific, well-defined, or rigid—instead of being neutral and open-ended—is unrealistic and potentially damaging. I define an unrealistic expectation as one that does not correspond with the possibilities available from the market's perspective. If each moment in the market is unique, and anything is possible, then any expectation that does not reflect these boundary-less characteristics is unrealistic.

MANAGING EXPECTATIONS

The potential damage caused by holding unrealistic expectations comes from how it affects the way we perceive information. Expectations are mental representations of what some future moment will look, sound, taste, smell, or feel like. Expectations come from what we know. This makes sense, because we can't expect something that we have no knowledge or awareness of. What we know is synonymous with what we have learned to believe about the ways in which the external environment can express itself. What we believe is our own personal version of the truth. When we expect something, we are projecting out into the future what we believe to be true. We are expecting the outside environment a minute, an hour, a day, a week, or a month from now to be the way we have represented it in our minds.

We have to be careful about what we project out into the future, because nothing else has the potential to create more unhappiness and emotional misery than an unfulfilled expectation. When things happen exactly as you expect them to, how do you feel? The response is generally wonderful (including feelings like happiness, joy, satisfaction, and a greater sense of well-being), unless, of course, you were expecting something dreadful and it manifested itself. Conversely, how do you feel when your expectations are not fulfilled? The universal response is emotional pain. Everyone experiences some degree of anger, resentment, despair, regret, disappointment, dissatisfaction, or betrayal when the environment doesn't turn out to be exactly as we expected it to be (unless, of course, we are completely surprised by something much better than we imagined).

Here's where we run into problems. Because our expectations come from what we know, when we decide or believe that we know something, we naturally expect to be right. At that point, we're no longer in a neutral or open state of mind, and it's not difficult to understand why. If we're going to feel great if the market does what we expect it to do, or feel horrible if it doesn't, then we're not exactly neutral or open-minded. Quite the contrary, the force of the belief behind the expectation will cause us to perceive market information in a way that confirms what we expect (we naturally like feeling good); and our pain-avoidance mechanisms will shield us from information that doesn't confirm what we expect (to keep us from feeling bad).

As I've already indicated, our minds are designed to help us avoid pain, both physical and emotional. These pain-avoidance mechanisms exist at both conscious and subconscious levels. For example, if an object is coming toward your head, you react instinctively to get out of the way. Ducking does not require a conscious decision-making process. On the other hand, if you clearly see the object and have time to consider the alternatives, you may decide to catch the object, bat it away with your hand, or duck. These are examples of how we protect ourselves from physical pain.

Protecting ourselves from emotional or mental pain works in the same way, except that we are now protecting ourselves from information. For example, the market expresses information about itself and its potential to move in a particular direction. If there's a difference between what we want or expect and what the market is offering or making available, then our pain-avoidance mechanisms kick in to compensate for the differences. As with physical pain, these mechanisms operate at both the conscious and subconscious levels.

To protect ourselves from painful information at the conscious level, we rationalize, justify, make excuses, willfully gather information that will neutralize the significance of the conflicting information, get angry (to ward off the conflicting information), or just plain lie to ourselves.

At the subconscious level, the pain-avoidance process is much more subtle and mysterious. At this level, our minds may block our ability to see other alternatives, even though in other circumstances we would be able to perceive them. Now, because they are in conflict with what we want or expect, our pain-avoidance mechanisms can make them disappear (as if they didn't exist). To illustrate this phenomenon, the best example is one I have already given you: We are in a trade where the market is moving against us. In fact, the market has established a trend in the opposite direction to what we want or expect. Ordinarily, we would have no problem identifying or perceiving this pattern if it weren't for the fact that the market was moving against our position. But the pattern loses its significance (becomes invisible) because we find it too painful to acknowledge.

To avoid the pain, we narrow our focus of attention and concentrate on information that keeps us out of pain, regardless of how insignificant or minute. In the meantime, the information that clearly indicates the presence of a trend and the opportunity to trade in the direction of that trend becomes invisible. The trend doesn't disappear from physical reality, but our ability to perceive it does. Our pain-avoidance mechanisms block our ability to define and interpret what the market is doing as a trend.

The trend will then stay invisible until the market either reverses in our favor or we are forced out of the trade because the pressure of losing too much money becomes unbearable. It's not until we are either out of the trade or out of danger that the trend becomes apparent, as well as all the opportunities to make money by trading in the direction of the trend. This is a perfect example of 20-20 hindsight.

All the distinctions that would otherwise be perceivable become perfectly clear, after the fact, when there is no longer anything for our minds to protect us from.

We all have the potential to engage in self-protective pain-avoidance mechanisms, because they're natural functions of the way our minds operate. There may be times when we are protecting ourselves from information that has the potential to bring up deep-seated emotional wounds or trauma that we're just not ready to face, or don't have the appropriate skills or resources to deal with. In these cases, our natural mechanisms are serving us well. But more often, our pain-avoidance mechanisms are just protecting us from information that would indicate that our expectations do not correspond with what is available from the environment's perspective. This is where our pain-avoidance mechanisms do us a disservice, especially as traders.

To understand this concept, ask yourself what exactly about market information is threatening. Is it threatening because the market actually expresses negatively charged information as an inherent characteristic of the way it exists? It may seem that way, but at the most fundamental level, what the market gives us to perceive are up-tics and down-tics or up-bars and down-bars. These up and down tics form patterns that represent edges. Now, are any of these tics or the patterns they form negatively charged? Again, it may certainly seem that way, but from the market's perspective the information is neutral. Each up-tic, down-tic, or pattern is just information, telling us the market's position. If any of this information had a negative charge as an inherent characteristic of the way it exists, then wouldn't everyone exposed to it experience emotional pain?

For example, if both you and I get hit on the head with a solid object, there probably wouldn't be much difference in how we would feel. We'd both be in pain. Any part of our bodies coming into contact with a solid object with some degree of force will cause anyone with a normal nervous system to experience pain. We share the experience because our bodies are constructed in basically the same way. The pain is an automatic physiological response to the impact with a tangible object. Information in the form of words or gestures expressed by the environment, or up and down tics expressed by the market, can be just as painful as being hit with a solid object; but there's an important difference between information and objects. Information is not tangible. Information doesn't consist of atoms and molecules. To experience the potential effects of information, whether negative or positive, requires an interpretation.

The interpretations we make are functions of our unique mental frameworks. Everyone's mental framework is unique for two fundamental reasons. First, all of us were born with different genetically encoded behavior and personality characteristics that cause us to have different needs from one another. How positively or negatively and to what degree the environment responds to these needs creates experiences unique to each individual. Second, everyone is exposed to a variety of environmental forces. Some of these forces are similar from one individual to the next, but none are exactly the same.

If you consider the number of possible combinations of genetically encoded personality characteristics we can be born with, in relation to the almost infinite variety of environmental forces we can encounter throughout our lives, all of which contribute to the construction of our mental framework, then it's not difficult to see why there is no universal mental framework common to everyone. Unlike our bodies, which have a common molecular structure that experiences physical pain, there is no universal mind-set to assure us that we will share the potential negative or positive effects of information in the same way.

For example, someone could be projecting insults at you, intending to cause you to feel emotional pain. From the environment's perspective, this is negatively charged information. Will you experience the intended negative effects? Not necessarily! You have to be able to interpret the information as negative to experience it as negative. What if this person is insulting you in a language you don't understand, or is using words you don't know the meaning of? Would you feel the intended pain? Not until you built a framework to define and understand the words in a derogatory way. Even then, we can't assume that what you'd feel would correspond to the intent behind the insult. You could have a framework to perceive the negative intent, but instead of feeling pain, you might experience a perverse type of pleasure. I've encountered many people who, simply for their own amusement, like to get people riled up with negative emotions. If they happen to be insulted in the process, it creates a sense of joy because then they know how successful they've been.

A person expressing genuine love is projecting positively charged information into the environment. Let's say the intent behind the expression of these positive feelings is to convey affection, endearment, and friendship. Are there any assurances that the person or persons this positively charged information is being projected toward will interpret and experience it as such? No, there aren't. A person with a very low sense of self-esteem, or someone who experienced a great deal of hurt and disappointment in relationships, will often misinterpret an expression of genuine love as something else. In the case of a person with low self-esteem, if he doesn't believe he deserves to be loved in such a way, he will find it difficult, if not impossible, to interpret what he is being offered as genuine or real. In the second case, where one has a significant backlog of hurt and disappointment in relationships, a person could easily come to believe that a genuine expression of love is extremely rare, if not non-existent, and would probably interpret the situation either as someone wanting something or trying to take advantage of him in some way.

I'm sure that I don't have to go on and on, sighting examples of all the possible ways there are to misinterpret what someone is trying to communicate to us or how what we express to someone can be misconstrued and experienced in ways completely unintended by us. The point that I am making is that each individual will define, interpret, and consequently experience whatever information he is exposed to in his own unique way. There's no standardized way to experience what the environment may be offering—whether it's positive, neutral, or negative information—simply because there is no standardized mental framework in which to perceive information.

Consider that, as traders, the market offers us something to perceive at each moment. In a sense, you could say that the market is communicating with us. If we start out with the premise that the market does not generate negatively charged information as an inherent characteristic of the way it exists, we can then ask, and answer, the question, "What causes information to take on a negative quality?" In other words, where exactly does the threat of pain come from?

If it's not coming from the market, then it has to be coming from the way we define and interpret the available information. Defining and interpreting information is a function of what we assume we know or what we believe to be true. If what we know or believe is in fact true—and we wouldn't believe it if it weren't—then when we project our beliefs out into some future moment as an expectation, we naturally expect to be right.

When we expect to be right, any information that doesn't confirm our version of the truth automatically becomes threatening. Any information that has the potential to be threatening also has the potential to be blocked, distorted, or diminished in significance by our pain-avoidance mechanisms. It's this particular characteristic of the way our minds function that can really do us a disservice. As traders, we can't afford to let our pain-avoidance mechanisms cut us off from what the market is communicating to us about what is available in the way of the next opportunity to get in, get out, add to, or subtract from a position, just because it's doing something that we don't want or expect.

For example, when you're watching a market (one you rarely, if ever, trade in) with no intention of doing anything, do any of the up or down tics cause you to feel angry, disappointed, frustrated, disillusioned, or betrayed in any way? No! The reason is that there's nothing at stake. You're simply observing information that tells you where the market is at that moment. If the up and down tics that you're watching form into some sort of behavior pattern you've learned to identify, don't you readily recognize and acknowledge the pattern? Yes, for the same reason: There's nothing at stake.

There is nothing at stake because there's no expectation. You haven't projected what you believe, assume, or think you know about that market into some future moment. As a result, there's nothing to be either right about or wrong about, so the information has no potential to take on a threatening or negatively charged quality. With no particular expectation, you haven't placed any boundaries on how the market can express itself. Without any mental boundaries, you will be making yourself available to perceive everything you've learned about the nature of the ways in which the market moves. There's nothing for your pain-avoidance mechanisms to exclude, distort, or diminish from your awareness in order to protect you.

In my workshops, I always ask participants to resolve the following primary trading paradox: In what way does a trader have to learn how to be rigid and flexible at the same time? The answer is: We have to be rigid in our rules and flexible in our expectations. We need to be rigid in our rules so that we gain a sense of self-trust that can, and will always, protect us in an environment that has few, if any, boundaries. We need to be flexible in our expectations so we can perceive, with the greatest degree of clarity and objectivity, what the market is communicating to us from its perspective. At this point, it probably goes without saying that the typical trader does just the opposite: He is flexible in his rules and rigid in his expectations. Interestingly enough, the more rigid the expectation, the more he has to either bend, violate, or break his rules in order to accommodate his unwillingness to give up what he wants in favor of what the market is offering.

ELIMINATING THE EMOTIONAL RISK

To eliminate the emotional risk of trading, you have to neutralize your expectations about what the market will or will not do at any given moment or in any given situation. You can do this by being willing to think from the market's perspective. Remember, the market is always communicating in probabilities. At the collective level, your edge may look perfect in every respect; but at the individual ic. every trader who has the potential to act as a force on price movement can negate the positive outcome of that edge.

To think in probabilities, you have to create a mental framework or mind-set that is consistent with the underlying principles of a probabilistic environment. A probabilistic mind-set pertaining to trading consists of five fundamental truths.

1. Anything can happen.

2. You don't need to know what is going to happen next in order to make money.

3. There is a random distribution between wins and losses for any given set of variables that define an edge.

4. An edge is nothing more than an indication of a higher probability of one thing happening over another.

5. Every moment in the market is unique.

Keep in mind that your potential to experience emotional pain comes from the way you define and interpret the information you're exposed to. When you adopt these five truths, your expectations will always be in line with the psychological realities of the market environment. With the appropriate expectations, you will eliminate your potential to define and interpret market information as either painful or threatening, and you thereby effectively neutralize the emotional risk of trading.

The idea is to create a carefree state of mind that completely accepts the fact that there are always unknown forces operating in the market. When you make these truths a fully functional part of your belief system, the rational part of your mind will defend these truths in the same way it defends any other belief you hold about the nature of trading. This means that, at least at the rational level, your mind will automatically defend against the idea or assumption that you can know for sure what will happen next. It's a contradiction to believe that each trade is a unique event with an uncertain outcome and random in relationship to any other trade made in the past; and at the same time to believe you know for sure what will happen next and to expect to be right.

If you really believe in an uncertain outcome, then you also have to expect that virtually anything can happen. Otherwise, the moment you let your mind hold onto the notion that you *know*, you stop taking all of the unknown variables into consideration. Your mind won't let you have it both ways. If you believe you know something, the moment is no longer unique. If the moment isn't unique, then everything is known or knowable; that is, there's nothing not to know. However, the moment you stop factoring in what you don't or can't know about the situation instead of being available to perceive what the market *is* offering, you make yourself susceptible to all of the typical trading errors.

For example, if you really believed in an uncertain outcome, would you ever consider putting on a trade without defining your risk in advance? Would you ever hesitate to cut a loss, if you really believed you didn't know? What about trading errors like jumping the gun? How could you anticipate a signal that hasn't yet manifested itself in the market, if you weren't convinced that you were going to miss out?

Why would you ever let a winning trade turn into a loser, or not have a systematic way of taking profits, if you weren't convinced the market was going your way indefinitely? Why would you hesitate to take a trade or not put it on at all, unless you were convinced that it was a loser when the market was at your original entry point? Why would you break your money management rules by trading too large a position relative to your equity or emotional tolerance to sustain a loss, if you weren't positive that you had a sure thing?

Finally, if you really believed in a random distribution between wins and losses, could you ever feel betrayed by the market? If you flipped a coin and guessed right, you wouldn't necessarily expect to be right on the next flip simply because you were right on the last. Nor would you expect to be wrong on the next flip if you were wrong on the last. Because you believe in a random distribution between the sequence of heads and tails, your expectations would be perfectly aligned with the reality of the situation. You would certainly like to be right, and if you were that would be great, but if you were wrong then you would not feel betrayed by the flip, because you know and accept that there are unknown variables at work that affect the outcome. Unknown means "not something your rational thinking process can take into consideration in advance of the flip," except to fully accept that you don't know. As a result, there is little, if any, potential to experience the kind of emotional pain that wells up when you feel betrayed.

As a trader, when you're expecting a random outcome, you will always be at least a little surprised at whatever the market does— even if it conforms exactly to your definition of an edge and you end up with a winning trade. However expecting a random outcome doesn't mean that you can't use your full reasoning and analytical abilities to project an outcome, or that you can't guess what's going to happen next, or have a hunch or feeling about it, because you can. Furthermore, you can be right in each instance. You just can't *expect* to be right. And if you are right, you can't expect that whatever you did that worked the last time will work again the next time, even though the situation may look, sound, or feel exactly the same.

Anything that you are perceiving "now" in the market will never be exactly the same as some previous experience that exists in your mental environment. But that doesn't mean that your mind (as a natural characteristic of the way it functions) won't try to make the two identical. There will be similarities between the "now moment" and something that you know from the past, but those similarities only give you something to work with by putting the odds of success in your favor. If you approach trading from the perspective that you don't know what will happen next, you will circumvent your mind's natural inclination to make the "now moment" identical to some earlier experience. As unnatural as it seems to do so, you can't let some previous experience (either negative or extremely positive) dictate your state of mind. If you do, it will be very difficult, if not impossible, to perceive what the market is communicating from its perspective.

When I put on a trade, all I expect is that something will happen. Regardless of how good I think my edge is, I expect nothing more than for the market to move or to express itself in some way. However, there are some things that I do know for sure. I know that based on the market's past behavior, the odds of it moving in the direction of my trade are good or acceptable, at least in relationship to how much I am willing to spend to find out if it does.

I also know before getting into a trade how much I am willing to let the market move against my position. There is always a point at which the odds of success are greatly diminished in relation to the profit potential. At that point, it's not worth spending any more money to find out if the trade is going to work. If the market reaches that point, I know without any doubt, hesitation, or internal conflict that I will exit the trade. The loss doesn't create any emotional damage, because I don't interpret the experience negatively. To me, losses are simply the cost of doing business or the amount of money I need to spend to make myself available for the winning trades. If, on the other hand, the trade turns out to be a winner, in most cases I know for sure at what point I am going to take my profits. (If I don't know for sure, I certainly have a very good idea.)

The best traders are in the "now moment" because there's no stress. There's no stress because there's nothing at risk other than the amount of money they are willing to spend on a trade. They are not trying to be right or trying to avoid being wrong; neither are they trying to prove anything. If and when the market tells them that their edges aren't working or that it's time to take profits, their minds do nothing to block this information. They completely accept what the market is offering them, and they wait for the next edge.

CHAPTER 8

WORKING WITH YOUR BELIEFS

Now the task before you is to properly integrate the five fundamental truths presented in Chapter 7 in your mental environment at a functional level. To help you do that, we will take an in-depth look at beliefs— their nature, properties, and characteristics. However, before we do that I will review and organize the major concepts presented thus far into a much clearer and more practical framework. What you learn from this and the next two chapters will form the foundation for understanding everything you need to do to achieve your goals as a trader.

DEFINING THE PROBLEM

At the most fundamental level, the market is simply a series of up and down tics that form patterns. Technical analysis defines these patterns as edges. Any particular pattern defined as an edge is simply an indication that there is a higher probability that the market will move in one direction over the other. However, there is a major mental paradox here because a pattern implies consistency, or, at least, a consistent outcome. But the reality is each pattern is a unique occurrence. They may look (or measure) exactly the same from one occurrence to the next, but the similarities are only on the surface. The underlying force behind each pattern is traders, and the traders who contribute to the formation of one pattern are always different from the traders who contribute to the next; so the outcome of each pattern is random relative to one another. Our minds have an inherent design characteristic (the association mechanism) that can make this paradox difficult to deal with.

Now these edges, or the patterns they represent, flow by in every time frame, making the market a never-ending stream of opportunities to get in, get out (scratch a trade), take profits, cut losses, or add to or detract from a position. In other words, from the market's perspective, each moment presents each one of us traders with the opportunity to do something on our own behalf.

What prevents us from perceiving each "now moment" as an opportunity to do something for ourselves or to act appropriately even when we do? Our fears! What is the source of our fears? We know its not the market, because from the market's perspective, the up and down tics and the patterns they create are neither positively or negatively charged. As a result, the up and down tics themselves have no capacity to cause us to enter into any particular state of mind (negative or positive), lose our objectivity, make errors, or take us out of the opportunity flow.

If it's not the market that causes us to experience a negatively charged state of mind, then what does cause it? The way we define and interpret the information we perceive. If that's the case, then what determines what we perceive and how we define and interpret that information? What we believe or what we assume to be true. Our beliefs working in conjunction with the association and pain-avoidance mechanisms act as a force on our five senses, causing us to perceive, define, and interpret market information in a way that is consistent with what we expect. What we expect is synonymous with what we believe or assume to be true. Expectations are beliefs projected into some future moment.

Each moment from the market's perspective is unique; but if the information being generated by the market is similar in quality, properties, or characteristic to something that is already in our minds, the two sets of information (outside and inside) automatically become linked. When this connection is made, it triggers a state of mind (confidence, euphoria, fear, terror, disappointment, regret, betrayal, etc.) that corresponds to whatever belief, assumption, or memory the outside information was linked to. This makes it *seem as if* what is outside is exactly the same as whatever is already inside of us.

It's our state of mind that makes the truth of whatever we're perceiving outside of us (in the market) seem indisputable and beyond question. Our state of mind is always the absolute truth. If I feel confident, then I am confident. If I feel afraid, then I am afraid. We can't dispute the quality of energy flowing through our mind and body at any given moment. And because I *know* as an indisputable fact how I feel, you could say that I also know the truth of what I'm perceiving outside of me in the same moment. The problem is that how we feel is always the absolute truth, but the beliefs that triggered our state of mind or feeling may or may not be true relative to the possibilities that exist in the market at any given moment.

Recall the example of the boy and the dog. The boy "knew" for an absolute fact that each dog he encountered after the first was threatening, because of the way he felt when one came into his field of awareness. These other dogs did not cause his fear; his negatively charged memory working in conjunction with the association and his pain-avoidance mechanism caused his fear. He experienced his own version of the truth, which did not correspond with the possibilities that existed from the environment's perspective. His belief about the nature of dogs was limited relative to the possible characteristics and traits expressed by dogs. Yet the state of mind he experienced every rienced every time he encountered a dog caused him to believe that he "knew" exactly what to expect from them.

This same process causes us to believe that we "know" exactly what to expect from the market, when the reality is there are always unknown forces operating at every moment. The trouble is, the instant we think we "know" what to expect, we simultaneously stop taking all the unknown forces and the various possibilities created by those forces into consideration. The unknown forces are other traders waiting to enter or exit trades, based on their beliefs about the future. In other words, we really can't know exactly what to expect from the market, until we can read the minds of all the traders who have the potential to act as a force on price movement. Not a very likely possibility.

As traders, we can't afford to indulge ourselves in any form of "I know what to expect from the market." We can "know" exactly what an edge looks, sounds, or feels like, and we can "know" exactly how much we need to risk to find out if that edge is going to work. We can "know" that we have a specific plan as to how we are going to take profits if a trade works. *But that's it!* If what we think we know starts expanding to what the market is going to do, we're in trouble. And all that's required to put us into a negatively charged, "I know what to expect from the market" state of mind is for any belief, memory, or attitude to cause us to interpret the up and down tics or any market information as anything but an opportunity to do something on our own behalf.

DEFINING THE TERMS

What Are the Objectives?

Ultimately, of course, making money is everyone's objective. But if trading were only a matter of making money, reading this book wouldn't be necessary. Putting on a winning trade or even a series of winning trades requires absolutely no skill. On the other hand, creating consistent results and being able to keep what we've created does require skill. Making money consistently is a by-product of acquiring and mastering certain mental skills. The degree to which you understand this is the same degree to which you will stop focusing on the money and focus instead on how you can use your trading as a tool to master these skills.

What Are the Skills?

Consistency is the result of a carefree, objective state of mind, where we are making ourselves available to perceive and act upon whatever the market is offering us (from its perspective) in any given "now moment."

What Is a Carefree State of Mind?

Carefree means confident, but not euphoric. When you are in a carefree state of mind, you won't feel any fear, hesitation, or compulsion to do anything, because you've effectively eliminated the potential to define and interpret market information as threatening. To remove the sense of threat, you have to accept the risk completely. When you have accepted the risk, you will be at peace with any outcome. To be at peace with any outcome, you must reconcile anything in your mental environment that conflicts with the five fundamental truths about the market. What's more, you also have to integrate these truths into your mental system as core beliefs.

What Is Objectivity?

Objectivity is a state of mind where you have conscious access to everything you have learned about the nature of market movement. In other words, nothing is being blocked or altered by your pain-avoidance mechanisms.

What Does it Mean to Make Yourself Available?

Making yourself available means trading from the perspective that you have nothing to prove. You aren't trying to win or to avoid losing. You aren't trying get your money back or to take revenge on the market. In other words, you come to the market with no agenda other than to let it unfold in any way that it chooses and to be in the best state of mind to recognize and take advantage of the opportunities it makes available to you.

What Is the "Now Moment"?

Trading in the "now moment" means that there is no potential to associate an opportunity to get into, get out of, add too, or detract from a trade with a past experience that already exists in your mental environment.

HOW THE FUNDAMENTAL TRUTHS RELATE TO THE SKILLS

1. Anything can happen. Why? Because there are always unknown forces operating in every market at every moment, it takes only one trader somewhere in the world to negate the positive outcome of your edge. That's all: only one. Regardless of how much time, effort, or money you've invested in your analysis, from the market's perspective there are no exceptions to this truth. Any exceptions that may exist in your mind will be a source of conflict and potentially cause you to perceive market information as threatening.

2. You don't need to know what is going to happen next in order to make money. Why? Because there is a random distribution between wins and losses for any given set of variables that define an edge. (See number 3.) In other words, based on the past performance of your edge, you may know that out of the next 20 trades, 12 will be winners and 8 will be losers. What you don't know is the sequence of wins and losses or how much money the market is going to make available on the winning trades. This truth makes trading a probability or numbers game. When you really believe that trading is simply a probability game, concepts like right and wrong or win and lose no longer have the same significance. As a result, your expectations will be in harmony with the possibilities.

Keep in mind that nothing has more potential to cause emotional discord than our unfulfilled expectations. Emotional pain is the universal response when the outside world expresses itself in a way that doesn't reflect what we expect or believe to be true. As a result, any market information that does not confirm our expectations is automatically defined and interpreted as threatening. That interpretation causes us to adopt a negatively charged, defensive state of mind, where we end up creating the very experience we are trying to avoid.

Market information is only threatening if you are expecting the market to do something for you. Otherwise, if you don't expect the market to make you right, you have no reason to be afraid of being wrong. If you don't expect the market to make you a winner, you have no reason to be afraid of losing. If you don't expect the market to keep going in your direction indefinitely, there is no reason to leave money on the table. Finally, if you don't expect to be able to take advantage of every opportunity just because you perceived it and it presented itself, you have no reason to be afraid of missing out.

On the other hand, if you believe that all you need to know is:

1. the odds are in your favor before you put on a trade;

2. how much it's going to cost to find out if the trade is going to work;

3. you don't need to know what's going to happen next to make money on that trade; and

4. anything can happen;

Then how can the market make you wrong? What information could the market generate about itself that would cause your pain-avoidance mechanisms to kick in so that you exclude that information from your awareness? None that I can think of. If you believe that anything can happen and that you don't need to know what is going to happen next to make money, then you will always be right. Your expectations will always be in harmony with the conditions as they exist from the market's perspective, effectively neutralizing your potential to experience emotional pain.

By the same token, how can a losing trade or even a series of losers have the typical negative effect, if you really believe that trading is a probability or numbers game? If your edge puts the odds in your favor, then every loss puts you that much closer to a win. When you really believe this, your response to a losing trade will no longer take on a negative emotional quality.

3. There is a random distribution between wins and losses for any given set of variables that define an edge. If every loss puts you that much closer to a win, you will be looking forward to the next occurrence of your edge, ready and waiting to jump in without the slightest reservation or hesitation. On the other hand, if you still believe that trading is about analysis or about being right, then after a loss you will anticipate the occurrence of your next edge with trepidation, wondering if it's going to work. This, in turn, will cause you to start gathering evidence for or against the trade. You will gather evidence for the trade if your fear of missing out is greater than your fear of losing. And you will gather information against the trade if your fear of losing is greater than your fear of missing out. In either case, you will not be in the most conducive state of mind to produce consistent results.

4. An edge is nothing more than an indication of a higher probability of one thing happening over another. Creating consistency requires that you completely accept that trading isn't about hoping, wondering, or gathering evidence one way or the other to determine if the next trade is going to work. The only evidence you need to gather is whether the variables you use to define an edge are present at any given moment. When you use "other" information, outside the parameters of your edge to decide whether you will take the trade, you are adding random variables to your trading regime.

Adding random variables makes it extremely difficult, if not impossible, to determine what works and what doesn't. If you're never certain about the viability of your edge, you won't feel too confident about it. To whatever degree you lack confidence, you will experience fear. The irony is, you will be afraid of random, inconsistent results, without realizing that your random, inconsistent approach is creating exactly what you are afraid of.

On the other hand, if you believe that an edge is simply a higher probability of one thing happening over another, and there's a random distribution between wins and losses for any given set of variables that define an edge, why would you gather "other" evidence for or against a trade? To a trader operating out of these two beliefs, gathering "other" evidence wouldn't make any sense. Or let me put it this way: Gathering "other" evidence makes about as much sense as trying to determine whether the next flip of a coin will be heads, after the last ten flips came up tails. Regardless of what evidence you find to support heads coming up, there is still a 50-percent chance that the next flip will come up tails. By the same token, regardless of how much evidence you gather to support acting or not acting on a trade, it still only takes one trader somewhere in the world to negate the validity of any, if not all, of your evidence. The point is *why bother!* If the market is offering you a legitimate edge, determine the risk and take the trade.

5. Every moment in the market is unique. Take a moment and think about the concept of uniqueness. "Unique" means not like anything else that exists or has ever existed. As much as we may understand the concept of uniqueness, our minds don't deal with it very well on a practical level. As we have already discussed, our minds are hardwired to automatically associate (without conscious awareness) anything in the exterior environment that is similar to anything that is already inside of us in the form of a memory, belief, or attitude. This creates an inherent contradiction between the way we naturally think about the world and the way the world exists. No two moments in the external environment will ever exactly duplicate themselves. To do so, every atom or every molecule would have to be in the exact same position they were in some previous moment. Not a very likely possibility. Yet, based on the way our minds are designed to process information, we will experience the "now moment" in the environment as being exactly the same as some previous moment as it exists inside our minds.

If each moment is like no other, then there's nothing at the level of your rational experience that can tell you for sure that you "know" what will happen next. So I will say again, why bother trying to know?! When you try to know, you are, in essence, trying to be right. I am not implying here that you can't predict what the market will do next and be right, because you most certainly can. It's in the trying that you run into all of the problems. If you believe that you correctly predicted the market once, you will naturally try to do it again. As a result, your mind will automatically start scanning the market for the same pattern, circumstance, or situation that existed the last time you correctly predicted its movement. When you find it, your state of mind will make it seem as if everything is exactly as it was the last time. The problem is that, from the market's perspective, it is not the same. As a result, you are setting yourself up for disappointment.

What separates the best traders from all the rest is that they have trained their minds to believe in the uniqueness of each moment (although this training usually takes the form of losing several fortunes before they "really" believe in the concept of uniqueness). This belief acts as a counteracting force, neutralizing the automatic association mechanism. When you truly believe that each moment is unique, then by definition there isn't anything in your mind for the association mechanism to link that moment to. This belief acts as an internal force causing you to disassociate the "now" moment in the market from any previous moment filed away in your mental environment. The stronger your belief in the uniqueness of each moment, the lower your potential to associate. The lower your potential to associate, the more open your mind will be to perceive what the market is offering you from its perspective.

Moving toward "the zone"

When you completely accept the psychological realities of the market, you will correspondingly accept the risks of trading. When you accept the risks of trading, you eliminate the potential to define market information in painful ways. When you stop defining and interpreting market information in painful ways, there is nothing for your mind to avoid, nothing to protect against. When there's nothing to protect against, you will have access to all that you know about the nature of market movement. Nothing will get blocked, which means you will perceive all the possibilities you have learned about (objectively), and since your mind is open to a true exchange of energy, you will quite naturally start discovering other possibilities (edges) that you formerly couldn't perceive.

For your mind to be open to a true exchange of energy, you can't be in a state of knowing or believing that you already know what's going to happen next. When you are at peace with not knowing what's going to happen next, you can interact with the market from a perspective where you will be making yourself available to let the market tell you, from its perspective, what is likely to happen next. At that point, you will be in the best state of mind to spontaneously enter "the zone," where you are tapped into the "now moment opportunity flow."

CHAPTER 9

THE NATURE OF
BELIEFS

At this point, if you can sense the benefits of adopting the five fundamental truths about trading, then the task is to learn how to properly integrate these truths into your mental system as core beliefs that are not in conflict with any other beliefs you may hold.

At first glance, this may seem like a daunting task and under other circumstances I would agree with you, but it won't be, because in Chapter 11 I'll give you a simple trading exercise specifically designed to properly install these truths as beliefs at a functional level. A functional level is, one where you find yourself just naturally operating out of a carefree state of mind, perceiving exactly what you need to do and doing it without hesitation or internal conflict.

However, I do have a word of caution for those of you who have already looked at the exercise. On the surface, the trading exercise looks so simple that you may be tempted to do it now, before you thoroughly understand the implications of what you are doing. I strongly suggest that you reconsider. There are some subtle yet profound dynamics involved in the process of learning how to install new beliefs and change any existing beliefs that are in conflict with the new ones. Understanding the trading exercise itself is easy. Understanding how to use the exercise to change your beliefs is another matter entirely. If you do the exercise without understanding the concepts presented in this chapter and the next, you will not achieve the desired results.

It is also important that you not take for granted the amount of mental effort you may have to expend to train your mind to fully accept these principles of success, regardless of how well you understand them. Remember Bob, the CTA who believed he thoroughly understood the concept of probabilities, but didn't have the ability to function from a probabilistic perspective.

Many people make the mistake of assuming that once they understand something, the insight inherent in their new understanding automatically becomes a functional part of their identity. Most of the time, understanding a concept is only a first step in the process of integrating that concept at a functional level. This is especially true of concepts that deal with thinking in probabilities. Our minds are not naturally wired to be "objective" or to stay in the "now moment." This means we have to actively train our minds to think from these perspectives.

In addition to the training involved, there may be any number of conflicting beliefs to work through. Conflicting beliefs will have the effect of sabotaging your best intentions to operate from an objective state of mind or to experience the "now moment opportunity flow." For example, let's say you've spent years learning how to read the markets, or spent large sums of money developing or buying technical systems, just so you could find out what was going to happen next. Now you have come to understand that you don't have to know what's going to happen next, and that even trying to know will detract from your ability to be objective or to stay in the moment. What we have is a direct conflict between your old belief that you need to know what will happen next to be successful and your new understanding that you don't need to know.

Now, will your new understanding suddenly neutralize all the time, money, and energy expended on reinforcing the belief that you "need to know"? I wish it were that easy. And for some lucky few, it may be. If you will recall in Chapter 4 when I talked about psychological distance in relationship to software code, I said that some traders may already be so close to these new perspectives that all they need is to put together a few of the missing pieces to create a mind-altering, "ah, ha" experience.

However, based on my experience of working with well over a thousand traders, I can say that most are not close to these perspectives at all. For those of you who are not, it may take a considerable amount of mental work (over a considerable amount of time) to properly integrate your new understandings about trading into your mental environment. The good news is that, ultimately, the exercise I present in Chapter 11 will install the five fundamental truths and resolve many of the potential conflicts, but only if you know exactly what you are doing and why you are doing it. That is the subject of this and the next chapter.

THE ORIGINS OF A BELIEF

What can we learn about the nature of beliefs, and how can we use that knowledge to create a mind-set that fosters our desire to be a consistently successful trader? These are the two questions I am going to focus on answering in this chapter.

First, let's look at the origin of our beliefs. As you may recall, memories, distinctions, and beliefs exist in the form of energy—specifically, structured energy. Earlier, I lumped these three mental components together to illustrate:

1. that memories, distinctions, and beliefs do not exist as physical matter;

2. that the cause-and-effect relationship that exists between ourselves and the external environment brings these components into existence; and

3. how the cause-and-effect relationship reverses so that we can perceive in the external environment what we have learned about.

To get at the origins of our beliefs, we're going to have to unbundle these components to illustrate the difference between a memory and a belief. The best way to do this is to imagine ourselves in the mind of an infant. I would think that at the very beginning of a child's life, the memories of his experiences would exist in their purest form. By that I mean that the memories of what he has seen, heard, smelled, touched, or tasted exist in his mind as pure sensory information that is not organized or attached to any specific words or concepts. Therefore, I am going to define a pure memory as sensory information stored in its original form.

A belief, on the other hand, is a concept about the nature of the way the external environment expresses itself. A concept combines pure sensory information with a symbol system we call language. For example, most infants have a pure memory of how it feels to be lovingly nurtured by a parent, but it isn't until the infant is taught to link or associate certain words with the pure sensory information stored in his memory that he will form a concept about how it feels to be lovingly nurtured.

The phrase "Life is wonderful" is a concept. By themselves, the words make up a meaningless collection of abstract symbols. But if a child is either taught or decides to connect these words to his positively charged feelings of being nurtured, then the letters are no longer a collection of abstract symbols and the words are no longer an abstract phrase. "Life is wonderful" becomes a definitive distinction about the nature of existence or the way the world works. By the same token, if the child didn't get enough nurturing, relative to his needs, he could just as easily link his feelings of emotional pain to a concept like "Life isn't fair" or "The world is an awful place."

In any case, when the positive or negative energy from our memories or experiences become linked to a set of words we call a concept, the concept becomes energized and, as a result, is transformed into a belief about the nature of reality. If you consider that concepts are structured by the framework of a language and energized by our experiences, it becomes clear why I refer to beliefs as "structured energy."

When a belief comes into existence, what does it do? What is its function? In some ways it seems ludicrous to ask those questions. After all, we all have beliefs. We are constantly expressing our beliefs both verbally and through our actions. Furthermore, we are constantly interacting with other people's beliefs as they express them. Yet, if I ask, "What exactly does a belief do?" chances are your mind will go blank.

On the other hand, if I were to ask about the functions of your eyes, ears, nose, or teeth, you would have no problem answering. Since beliefs are such important component parts of our make-up (in terms of their impact on the quality of our lives), it certainly has to be one of life's great ironies that they are also the least thought about and understood.

What I mean by "least thought about" is, if we have a problem with one of our body parts, we naturally focus our attention on that part and think about what we need to do to fix the problem. However, it doesn't necessarily occur to us that the problems we may be having with the quality of our lives (for example, lack of happiness, a sense of dissatisfaction, or lack of success in some area) are rooted in our beliefs.

This lack of consideration is a universal phenomenon. One of the prominent characteristics of beliefs is that they make what we experience seem self evident and beyond question. In fact, if it weren't for your intense desire to experience consistent success as a trader, it's unlikely you would be delving into this topic at all. Usually, it takes years of extreme frustration before people begin examining their beliefs as the source of their difficulties.

However, even though beliefs are an intricate part of our identity, you don't have to take this process of self analysis so personally. Consider the fact that none of us was born with any of our beliefs. They were all acquired in a combination of ways. Many of the beliefs that have the most profound impact on our lives were not even acquired by us as an act of free will. They were instilled by other people. And it probably won't come as a surprise to anyone that usually the beliefs that cause us the most difficulty are those that were acquired from others without our conscious consent. By that I mean beliefs that we acquired when we were too young and uninformed to realize the negative implications of what we were being taught.

Regardless of the source of our beliefs, once they are born into existence they all basically function in the same way. Beliefs have certain characteristic ways in which they do their jobs, not unlike the various parts of our bodies. For example, if you compare my eyes and your eyes, or my hands and your hands, or my red blood cells and your red blood cells, we can see that they are not exactly the same, but they have characteristics in common that cause them to function in similar ways. By the same token, a belief that "Life is wonderful" will perform its function in the same way as a belief that "Life is awful." The beliefs themselves are different and the effect that each has on the quality of the holder's life will be vastly different, but both beliefs will function in exactly the same manner.

BELIEFS AND THEIR IMPACT ON OUR LIVES

In the broadest sense, our beliefs shape the way we experience our lives. As I have already said, we're not born with any of our beliefs. They're acquired, and as they accumulate, we live our lives in a way that reflects what we have learned to believe. Consider how different your life would be if you had been born into a culture, religion, or political system that has very little, if anything, in common with the one you were born into. It might be hard to imagine, but what you would have learned to believe about the nature of life and how the world works may not be remotely similar to what you currently believe. Yet you would hold these other beliefs with the same degree of certainty as your current beliefs.

How Beliefs Shape Our Lives

1. They manage our perception and interpretation of environmental information in a way that is consistent with what we believe.

2. They create our expectations. Keep in mind that an expectation is a belief projected into some future moment. Since we can't expect something we don't know about, we could also say that an expectation is what we know projected into some future moment.

3. Anything we decide to do or any outward expression of behavior will be consistent with what we believe.

4. Finally, our beliefs shape how we feel about the results of our actions.

There isn't much about the way we function that beliefs don't play a major role in. So what I am going to do now is give you an example I used in my first book, *The Disciplined Trader*, to illustrate the various functions of a belief.

In the spring of 1987, I was watching a locally produced television program called "Gotcha Chicago." It was about some local celebrities who played practical jokes on one another. In one segment of the program, the TV station hired a man to stand on the sidewalk along Michigan Avenue holding a sign that read "Free money. Today only." (For those of you who are not familiar with Chicago, Michigan Avenue is home to many fashionable, exclusive department stores and boutiques.) The TV station gave the man a considerable amount of cash, with instructions to give money to anyone who asked for it.

Now, when you consider that Michigan Avenue is one of the busiest areas of the city, and if we assume that most of the people who passed the man on the street could read the sign, how many people would you think took him up on his offer and asked for some money? Of all the people who walked by and read the sign, only one person stopped, and said, "Great! May I have a quarter to buy a bus transfer?" Otherwise, no one would even go near the man.

Eventually, the man grew frustrated because people weren't reacting the way he expected them to. He started crying out, "Do you want any money? Please take my money; I can't give it away fast enough." Everyone just kept walking around him as if he didn't exist. In fact, I noticed that several people went out of their way to avoid him. As a man wearing a suit and carrying a briefcase approached, he went right up to him and said, "Would you like some money?" The man responded, "Not today." Really frustrated now, he shot back, "How many days does this happen? Would you please take this?" as he tried to hand the man some cash. The man responded with a terse "No" and walked on.

What was going on here? Why wouldn't anyone (except for the person who needed a bus transfer) ask for the money? If we assume that most or all of the passersby could read the sign, but still didn't make any effort to get the money, then one possible explanation for their behavior is that they just didn't care about money. This is extremely unlikely, though, considering how much of our lives is devoted to the pursuit of money.

If we agree that people could read the sign and that money is very important to most of us, then what could have stopped these people from helping themselves? The environment was making available an experience that most people would love to have: someone giving them money with no strings attached. Yet everyone walked by, oblivious to what was awaiting them. They must not have been able to perceive what was available. That's hard to imagine, because the sign clearly stated "Free money. Today only." However, it's not hard to imagine if you consider that most people have a belief (an energized concept about how the world works) that "Free money doesn't exist."

If free money really doesn't exist, then how does someone reconcile the obvious contradiction between that belief and the sign saying that it does? That's easy, just decide the man with the sign is crazy; what else could account for such bizarre behavior if, in fact, free money doesn't exist? The reasoning process that could compensate for the contradiction might go something like this: "Everyone knows getting money with no strings attached rarely happens. Certainly not from a stranger on one of the busiest streets in the city. In fact, if the man were really giving away money, he would already be mobbed. He might even be endangering his life. He must be crazy. I had better take a wide path around him; who knows what he might do?"

Notice that every component of the thought process described is consistent with the belief that free money doesn't exist.

1. The words "free money" were neither perceived nor interpreted as they were intended from the environment's perspective.

2. Deciding the person with the sign must be crazy created an expectation of danger, or at least a perception that caution was warranted.

3. Purposefully altering one's path to avoid the person with the sign is an action that is consistent with the expectation of danger.

4. How did each person feel about the outcome? That's difficult to say without knowing each person individually, but a good generalization would be that they felt relieved that they successfully avoided an encounter with a crazy person.

The feeling of relief that resulted from avoiding a confrontation is a state of mind. Remember that how we feel (the relative degree of positively or negatively charged energy flowing through our bodies and minds) is always the absolute truth. But the beliefs that prompt any particular state of mind may not be the truth with respect to the possibilities available from the environment's perspective.

Relief from confrontation was not the only possible outcome in this situation. Imagine how different the experience would be if they believed that "free money exists." The process described above would be the same, except it would make the belief that "free money exists," seem self-evident and beyond question, just as it made the belief that "free money doesn't exist," seem self-evident and beyond question.

A perfect example would be the one person who said "great, may I have a quarter for a bus transfer." When I saw this, I had the impression this guy was probably a panhandler and would have asked anybody for a quarter. A panhandler is someone who definitely believes in the existence of free money. Therefore, his perception and interpretation of the sign were exactly what was intended by the TV station. His expectation and behavior were consistent with his belief that free money exists. And how would he feel about the results? He got his quarter, so I would assume he felt a sense of satisfaction. Of course, what he didn't know is that he could have gotten a lot more.

There's another possible outcome for our scenario. Let's look at a hypothetical example of someone who believes that "free money doesn't exist," but who takes a "what if" approach to the situation. In other words, some people can be so intrigued and curious about the possibilities that they decide to temporarily suspend their belief that "free money doesn't exist." This temporary suspension allows them to act outside the boundaries created by a belief, in order to see what happens. So instead of ignoring the man with the sign, which would be our hypothetical person's first inclination, he walks up to him and says, "Give me ten dollars." The man promptly pulls a ten-dollar bill out of his pocket and gives it to him. What happens now? How does he feel, having experienced something unexpected that completely contradicted his belief?

For most people, the belief that free money doesn't exist is acquired through unpleasant circumstances, to put it mildly. The most common way is being told that we can't have something because it's too expensive. How many times does the typical child hear, "Who do you think you are anyway? Money doesn't grow on trees, you know." In other words, it is probably a negatively charged belief. So the experience of having money handed to him with no strings attached and without any negative comments would likely create a state of mind of pure elation.

In fact, most people would be so happy that they'd feel compelled to share that happiness and this new discovery with everyone they knew. I can imagine him going back to his office or going home, and the moment he encounters someone he knows, the first words that come out of his mouth will be, "You won't believe what happened to me today," and even though he desperately wants those he meets to believe his story, they probably won't. Why? Because their belief that free money doesn't exist will cause them to interpret his story in a way that negates its validity.

To take this example a little further, imagine what would happen to this person's state of mind if it occurred to him that he could have asked for more money. He is in a state of pure elation. However, the moment the thought either pops into his mind or someone he relates his story to offers the idea that he could have asked for a lot more money, his state of mind will immediately shift to a negatively charged state of regret or despair. Why? He tapped into a negatively charged belief about what it means to miss out on something or not get enough. As a result, instead of being happy over what he got, he will lament what he could have had but didn't get.

BELIEFS VS. THE TRUTH

In all three of these examples (including the hypothetical one), everybody experienced their own unique version of the situation. If asked, each person would describe what he or she experienced from their perspective, as if it were the only true and valid version of the reality of the situation. The contradiction between these three versions of the truth suggests to me a larger philosophical issue that needs to be resolved. If beliefs limit our awareness of the information being generated by the physical environment, so that what we perceive is consistent with whatever we believe, then how do we know what the truth is?

To answer this question, we have to consider four ideas:

1. The environment can express itself in an infinite combination of ways. When you combine all the forces of nature interacting with everything created by humans, then add to that the forces generated by all the possible ways people can express themselves, the result is a number of possible versions of reality that would surely overwhelm even the most open-minded person.

2. Until we have acquired the ability to perceive every possible way in which the environment can express itself, our beliefs will always represent a limited version of what is possible from the environment's perspective, making our beliefs a statement *about* reality, but not necessarily a definitive statement of reality.

3. If you find yourself taking exception to the second statement, then consider that if our beliefs were a true, 100-percent accurate reflection of physical reality, then our expectations would always be fulfilled. If our expectations were always fulfilled, we would be in a perpetual state of satisfaction. How could we feel other than happy, joyful, elated, and with a complete sense of well-being if physical reality was consistently showing up exactly as we expected it to?

4. If you can accept the third statement as being valid, then the corollary is also true. If we are not experiencing satisfaction, then we must be operating out of a belief or beliefs that don't work very well relative to the environmental conditions.

Taking these four ideas into consideration, I can now answer the question, "What is the truth?" The answer is, whatever works. If beliefs impose limitations on what we perceive as possible, and the environment can express itself in an infinite combination of ways, then beliefs can only be true relative to what we are attempting to accomplish at any given moment. In other words, the relative degree of truth inherent in our beliefs can be measured by how useful they are.

Each of us has internally generated forces (curiosity, needs, wants, desires, goals, and aspirations) that compel or motivate us to interact with the physical environment. The particular set of steps we take to fulfill the object of our curiosity, needs, wants, desires, goals, or aspirations is a function of what we believe to be true in any given circumstance or situation. That truth, whatever it is, will determine:

1. the possibilities we perceive in relation to what is available from the environment's perspective,

2. how we interpret what we perceive,

3. the decisions we make,

4. our expectations of the outcome,

5. the action we take, and

6. how we feel about the results of our efforts.

At any given moment, if we find ourselves in a state of satisfaction, happiness, or well-being in relation to whatever we are attempting to accomplish, we can say that our truth (meaning whatever beliefs we are operating from) are useful because the process, as stated above, worked. What we perceived was not only consistent with our objective, it was also consistent with what was available from the environment's perspective. Our interpretation of the information we perceived resulted in a decision, expectation, and action that were in harmony with the environmental situation and circumstance. There was no resistance or counteracting force offered by the environment (or in our own mind) that would diminish the outcome we were trying to achieve. As a result, we find ourselves in a state of satisfaction, happiness, and well-being.

On the other hand, if we find ourselves in a state of dissatisfaction, disappointment, frustration, confusion, despair, regret, or hopelessness, we can say that relative to the environmental situation and circumstances, the beliefs we are operating from don't work well or at all, and therefore are not useful. Simply put, the truth is a function of whatever works in relation to what we are trying to accomplish at any given moment.

CHAPTER 10

THE IMPACT OF BELIEFS ON TRADING

If the external environment can express itself in an infinite combination of ways, then there's really no limit to the number and types of beliefs available to be acquired about the nature of our existence. That is an elaborate way of saying that there's a lot out there to be learned about. Yet, to make a general observation about the nature of humanity, I would say that we certainly don't live our lives in a manner that is consistent with that statement. If it's true that it's possible to believe almost anything, then why are we always arguing and fighting with each other? Why isn't it all right for all of us to express our lives in a way that reflects what we have learned to believe?

There has to be something behind our relentless attempt to convince others of the validity of our beliefs and to deny the validity of theirs. Consider that every conflict, from the smallest to the largest, from the least to the most significant, whether between individuals, cultures, societies, or nations, is always the result of conflicting beliefs. What characteristics of our beliefs make us intolerant of divergent beliefs? In some cases, we are so intolerant that we are willing to kill each other to get our point across.

My personal theory is that beliefs are not only structured energy, but also energy that seems to be conscious, at least to the extent of having some degree of awareness. Otherwise, how can we account for our ability to recognize on the outside what is on the inside? How would we know our expectations are being fulfilled? How would we know when they are not? How would we know we are being confronted with information or circumstances that contradict what we believe? The only explanation I have is that each individual belief has to have some quality of either awareness or self-awareness that causes it to function as it does.

The idea of energy that has some degree of awareness may be difficult for many of you to accept. But there are several observations we can make about our individual and collective natures that support the possibility. First, everyone wants to be believed. It doesn't matter what the belief is; the experience of being believed feels good. I think these positive feelings are universal, meaning that they apply to everyone. Conversely, no one likes to be disbelieved; it doesn't feel good. If I said, "I don't believe you," the negative feeling that would resonate throughout your body and mind is also universal. By the same token, none of us likes to have our beliefs challenged. The challenge feels like an attack. Everyone, regardless of the belief, seems to respond in the same way: The typical response is to argue, defend ourselves (our beliefs), and, depending on the situation, attack back.

When expressing ourselves, we seem to like being listened to. If we sense our audience isn't paying attention, how does it feel? Not good! Again, I think this response is universal. Conversely, why is it so difficult to be a good listener? Because to be a good listener, we actually have to listen, without thinking about how we are going to express ourselves the moment we can either politely or rudely interrupt the person who's speaking. What's the compelling force behind our inability to listen without waiting to interrupt?

Don't we like being with people with similar beliefs, because it feels comfortable and secure? Don't we avoid people with dissimilar or conflicting beliefs, because it feels uncomfortable or even threatening? The bottom line implication is, the moment we acquire a belief, it seems to take on a life of its own, causing us to recognize and be attracted to its likeness and repelled by anything that is opposite or contradictory. Considering the vast number of divergent beliefs that exist, if these feelings of attraction or comfort and being repelled or threatened are universal, then each belief must somehow be conscious of its existence, and this conscious, structured energy must behave in characteristic ways that are common to all of us.

THE PRIMARY CHARACTERISTICS OF A BELIEF

There are three basic characteristics you need to understand in order to effectively install the five fundamental truths about trading at a functional level in your mental environment:

1. Beliefs seem to take on a life of their own and, therefore, resist any force that would alter their present form.

2. All active beliefs demand expression.

3. Beliefs keep on working regardless of whether or not we are consciously aware of their existence in our mental environment.

1. Beliefs resist any force that would alter their present form. We may not understand the underlying dynamics of how beliefs maintain their structural integrity, but we can observe that they do so, even in the face of extreme pressure or force. Throughout human history, there are many examples of people whose belief in some issue or cause was so powerful that they chose to endure indignities, torture, and death rather than express themselves in a way that violated their beliefs. This is certainly a demonstration of just how powerful beliefs can be and the degree to which they can resist any attempt to be altered or violated in the slightest way.

Beliefs seem to be composed of a type of energy or force that naturally resists any other force that would cause them to exist in any form other than their present form. Does this mean that they can't be altered? Absolutely not! It just means that we have to understand how to work with them. Beliefs can be altered, but not in the way that most people may think. I believe that once a belief has been formed, it cannot be destroyed. In other words, there is nothing we can do that would cause one or more of our beliefs to cease to exist or to evaporate as if they never existed at all. This assertion is founded in a basic law of physics. According to Albert Einstein and others in the scientific community, energy can neither be created nor destroyed; it can only be transformed. If beliefs are energy—structured, conscious energy that is aware of its existence—then this same principle of physics can be applied to beliefs, meaning, if we try to eradicate them, it's not going to work.

If you knew someone or something was trying to destroy you, how would you respond? You would defend yourself, fight back, and possibly become even stronger than you were before you knew of the threat. Each individual belief is a component of what we consider to be our identity. Isn't it reasonable to expect that, if threatened, each individual belief would respond in a way that was consistent with how all the parts respond collectively?

The same principle holds true if we try to act as if a particularly troublesome belief doesn't exist. If you woke up one morning and everyone you knew ignored you and acted as if you didn't exist, how would you respond? It probably wouldn't be long before you grabbed someone and got right in their face to try to force them to acknowledge you. Again, if purposely ignored, each individual belief will act in the very same way. It will find a way to force its presence into our conscious thought process or behavior.

The easiest and most effective way to work with our beliefs is to gently render them inactive or nonfunctional by drawing the energy out of them. I call this process de-activation. After de-activation, the original structure of the belief remains intact, so technically it hasn't changed. The difference is that the belief no longer has any energy. Without energy, it doesn't have the potential to act as a force on our perception of information or on our behavior.

Here is a personal illustration: As a young child, I was taught to believe in both Santa Claus and the Tooth Fairy. In my mental system, both of these are perfect examples of what are now inactive, nonfunctional beliefs. However, even though they are inactive, they still exist inside my mental system, only now they exist as concepts with no energy. If you recall from the last chapter, I defined beliefs as a combination of sensory experience and words that form an energized concept. The energy can be drawn out of the concept, but the concept itself remains intact, in its original form. However, without energy, it no longer has the potential to act on my perception of information or on my behavior.

So, as I'm sitting here typing into my computer, if someone came up to me and said that Santa Claus was at the door, how do you think I would define and interpret this information? I would treat it as being irrelevant or a joke, of course. However, if I were five years old and my mother told me that Santa Claus was at the front door, her words would have instantly tapped me into a huge reservoir of positively charged energy that would have compelled me to jump up and run to the front door as fast as I could. Nothing would have been able to stop me. I would have overcome any obstacle in my path.

At some point, my parents told me Santa Claus didn't exist. Of course, my first reaction was disbelief. I didn't believe them, nor did I want to believe them. Eventually, they convinced me. However, the process of convincing me did not destroy my belief in Santa Claus or cause it not to exist any longer; it just took all the energy out of the belief. The belief was transformed into a nonfunctional, inactive concept about how the world works. I'm not sure where all that energy went, but I know that some of it was transferred to a belief that Santa Claus doesn't exist. Now I have two contradictory distinctions about the nature of the world that exist in my mental system: one, Santa exists; two, Santa doesn't exist. The difference between them is in the amount of energy they contain. The first has virtually no energy; the second has energy. So from a functional perspective, there is no contradiction or conflict.

I propose that, if it's possible to render one belief inactive, then it's possible to de-activate any belief, despite the fact that all beliefs seem to resist any force that would alter their present form. The secret to effectively changing our beliefs is in understanding and, consequently, believing that we really aren't changing our beliefs; we are simply transferring energy from one concept to another concept, one that we find more useful in helping us to fulfill our desires or achieve our goals.

2. All active beliefs demand expression. Beliefs fall into two basic categories: active and inactive. The distinction between the two is simple. Active beliefs are energized; they have enough energy to act as a force on our perception of information and on our behavior. An inactive belief is just the opposite. It is a belief, that for any number of reasons, no longer has energy, or has so little energy that it's no longer able to act as a force on how we perceive information or how we express ourselves.

When I say that all active beliefs demand expression, I don't mean to imply that every belief in our mental environment is demanding to express itself simultaneously. For example, if I ask you to think about what's wrong with the world today, the word "wrong" would bring to your mind ideas about the nature of the world that reflect what you believe to be troubling or disturbing. Unless, of course, there is nothing about the state of the world you find troubling. The point is, if there is something you do believe is wrong, you weren't necessarily thinking about those ideas before I asked the question; but the moment I did, your beliefs about these issues instantly moved to the forefront of your conscious thinking process. In effect, they demanded to be heard.

I say that beliefs "demand" to be expressed because once something causes us to tap into our beliefs, it seems as if we can't stop the flood of energy that's released. This is especially true of emotionally sensitive issues or beliefs we feel particularly passionate about. You might ask, "Why would I want to hold back expressing my beliefs?" There could be several reasons. Consider a scenario in which you're interacting with someone in a superior position to you at work, and this person is saying something that you completely disagree with, or even find utterly absurd. Will you express your truth or hold back? That will depend on the beliefs you have about what is proper in such a situation. If your beliefs dictate that speaking up would be inappropriate, and those beliefs have more energy than the ones that are being contradicted, then you'll probably hold back and not argue openly.

You might be looking at this person (the boss) and nodding your head in agreement. But is your mind in agreement? More to the point, is your mind silent? Absolutely not! Your position on the issues being presented are effectively countering each point the boss is making. In other words, your beliefs are still demanding expression, but they aren't being expressed externally (in the environment) because other beliefs are acting as a counteracting force. However, they will soon find a way to get out, won't they? As soon as you are out of the situation, you will probably find a way to "unload," or even spew out your side of the argument. You will probably describe what you had to endure to anyone you think will lend a sympathetic ear. This is an example of how our beliefs demand to be expressed when they are in conflict with the external environment.

But what happens when one or more of our beliefs are in conflict with our intents, goals, dreams, wants, or desires? The implications of such a conflict can have a profound effect on our trading. As we have already learned, beliefs create distinctions in how the external environment can express itself. Distinctions, by definition, are boundaries. Human consciousness, on the other hand, seems to be larger than the sum total of everything we have learned to believe. This "larger than" quality of human consciousness gives us the ability to think in any direction we choose, either inside or outside of the boundaries imposed by our beliefs. Thinking outside of the boundaries of our beliefs is commonly referred to as creative thinking. When we purposely choose to question a belief (question what we know), and sincerely desire an answer, we make our minds available to receive a "brilliant idea," "inspiration," or "solution" to the issue at hand.

Creativity, by definition, brings forth something that didn't previously exist. When we put our minds into a creative thinking mode, we will (by definition, automatically) receive ideas or thoughts that are outside of anything that already exists in our rational mind as a belief or memory. As far as I know, there is no consensus among artists, inventors, or the religious or scientific communities as to exactly where creatively generated information comes from. However, what I do know is that creativity seems to be limitless and without boundaries.

If there are any limits on the ways we can think, we certainly haven't found them yet. Consider the staggering pace at which technology has developed in the last 50 years alone. Every invention or development in the evolution of humanity was born in the minds of people who were willing to think outside the boundaries dictated by what they had learned to believe.

If all of us have the inherent ability to think creatively (and I believe that we do), then we also have the potential to encounter what I call a "creative experience." I define a creative experience as the experience of anything new or outside the boundaries imposed by our beliefs. It could be a new sight—something we've never seen before, but from the environment's perspective was always there. Or we could experience a new sound, smell, taste, or touch. Creative experiences, like creative thoughts, inspirations, hunches, and brilliant ideas, can occur as a surprise or can be the result of our conscious direction. In either case, when we experience them we can be confronted with a major psychological dilemma. A creative occurrence, whether in the form of a thought or an experience, can cause us to be attracted to or desire something that is in direct conflict with one or more of our beliefs.

To illustrate the point, let's return to the example of the boy and dog. Recall that the boy has had several painful experiences with dogs. The first experience was real from the environment's perspective. The others, however, were the result of how his mind processed information (based on the operation of the association and pain-avoidance mechanisms). The end result is that he experiences fear every time he encounters a dog. Let's suppose that the boy was a toddler when he had his first negatively charged experience. As he grows up and begins associating specific words and concepts with his memories, he will form a belief about the nature of dogs. It would be reasonable to assume that he adopted a belief something like, "All dogs are dangerous."

With the use of the word "all," the boy's belief is structured in a way that assures that he will avoid all dogs. He has no reason to question this belief, because every experience has confirmed and reinforced its validity. However, he (and everyone else on the planet) is susceptible to a creative experience. Under normal circumstances, the boy will do everything possible to make sure he does not encounter a dog. But what if something unexpected and unintended occurs?

Suppose the boy is walking with his parents and, as a result, feels safe and protected. Now, suppose he and his parents come to a blind corner and cannot see what is on the other side. They encounter a scene in which several children of about the same age as the boy are playing with some dogs and, furthermore, they are obviously having a great deal of fun. This is a creative experience. The boy is confronted with indisputable information that what he believes about the nature of dogs isn't true. What happens now?

First, the experience was not at the boy's conscious direction. He didn't make a decision to willingly expose himself to information that contradicted what he believed to be true. We might call this an inadvertent creative experience, because the external environment forced him to confront other possibilities that he didn't believe existed. Second, the experience of seeing other children playing with dogs and not getting hurt will throw his mind into a state of confusion. After the confusion wears off, meaning as he begins to accept the possibility that not all dogs are dangerous, several scenarios are possible.

Seeing other children his own age (with whom he could strongly identify) having such a great time playing with dogs could cause the boy to decide that he wants to be like the other children and have fun with dogs, too. If that's the case, this inadvertent creative encounter has caused him to become attracted to express himself in a way that he formerly didn't believe was possible (interacting with dogs). In fact, the notion was so impossible that it wouldn't have even occurred to him to consider it. Now, he not only considers it, he desires it.

Will he be able to express himself in a way that is consistent with his desire? The answer to this question is a matter of energy dynamics. There are two forces within the boy that are in direct conflict with each other, competing for expression: his belief that "all dogs are dangerous" and his desire to have fun and be like the other children. What he will do the next time he encounters a dog will be determined by which has more energy: his belief or his desire.

Given the intensity of the energy in his belief that "All dogs are dangerous," we can reasonably assume that his belief will have far more energy than his desire. If that's the case, then he will find his next encounter with a dog very frustrating. Even though he may want to touch or pet the dog, he'll find that he can't interact with it in any way. The word "all" in his belief will act as a paralyzing force, preventing him from fulfilling his desire. He might be well aware of the fact that the dog he wants to pet is not dangerous and won't hurt him; but he won't be able to pet it until the balance of energy tips in favor of his desire.

If the boy genuinely wants to interact with dogs, he will have to overcome his fear. This means that he will have to de-activate his belief that all dogs are dangerous so he can properly install a belief about dogs that is more consistent with his desire. We know that dogs can express themselves in a wide range of ways, from loving and gentle to mean and nasty. However, very few dogs on a percentage basis fall into the mean and nasty category. A good belief for the boy to adopt, then, would be something like, "Most dogs are friendly, but some can be mean and nasty." This belief would allow him to learn to recognize characteristics and behavior patterns that will tell him which dogs he can play with and which ones to avoid.

However, the larger issue is, how can the boy de-activate the "all" in the belief that "All dogs are dangerous" so he can overcome his fear? Remember that all beliefs naturally resist any force that would alter their present form, but, as I indicated above, the appropriate approach is not to try to alter the belief, but rather to draw the energy out of it and channel that energy into another belief that is better suited to our purposes. To de-activate the concept the word "all" represents, the boy will have to create a positively charged experience with a dog; at some point, he will have to step through his fear and touch one.

Doing this might require a great deal of effort on the boy's part over a considerable amount of time. Early in the process, his new realization about dogs might be strong enough only to allow him to be in the presence of a dog, at a distance, and not run away. However, each encounter with a dog, even at a distance, that doesn't result in a negative outcome will draw more and more of the negative energy out of his belief that "All dogs are dangerous." Eventually, each new positive experience will allow him to close the gap between himself and a dog, little by little, to the point that he can actually touch one. From an energy dynamics perspective, he will be able to touch a dog when his desire to do so is at least one degree greater in intensity than his belief that all dogs are dangerous. The moment he actually does touch a dog, it will have the effect of drawing most of the remaining negative energy out of the "all" concept and transfer it to a belief that reflects his new experience.

Although it's probably not that common, there are people who, for various reasons, are motivated enough to purposely put themselves through the above described process. However, they may not be consciously aware of the dynamics involved. People who work through a childhood fear of this magnitude usually do so somewhat haphazardly over a period of years, without knowing for sure exactly how they did it (unless they seek and get competent professional help). Later on, as adults, if they are asked or if they happen to encounter a situation that reminds them of their past (for instance, observing a child who is terrified of dogs), they typically characterize the process they went through as "I remember when I was afraid of dogs, but I grew out of it."

The end result of the first scenario was that the boy worked through his fear by de-activating his limiting belief about the nature of dogs. This allowed him to express himself in a way that he finds pleasing and that otherwise would have been impossible.

The second scenario that could result from the child's inadvertent creative experience with dogs is that he isn't attracted to the possibility of playing with a dog. In other words, he could not care less about being like the other children or interacting with dogs. In this case, his belief that all dogs are dangerous and his new realization that all dogs are not dangerous will exist in his mental environment as contradictory concepts. This is an example of what I call an active contradiction, when two active beliefs are in direct conflict with each other, both demanding expression. In this example, the first belief exists at a core level in the boy's mental environment, with a great deal of negatively charged energy. The second belief is at a more superficial level, and has very little positively charged energy.

The dynamics of this situation are interesting, and extremely important. We have stated that beliefs control our perception of information. Under normal circumstances, the boy would have been perceptually blinded to the possibility of interacting with dogs, but the experience of seeing other children playing with them created a positively charged concept in his mental environment that dogs are not all dangerous; some can be friendly. However, he hasn't done anything to de-activate the "all" in his belief that "All dogs are dangerous," and, as far as I know, beliefs have no capacity to de-activate themselves. As a result, beliefs exist in our mental environment from the moment they are born to the moment we die, unless we consciously take steps to de-activate them. However, in this scenario, the boy has no desire and consequently no motivation to step through his fear.

Therefore, the boy is left with an active contradiction where his minimally charged belief that not all dogs are dangerous gives him the ability to perceive the possibility of playing with a dog, but his powerfully charged belief that all dogs are dangerous still causes him to experience some level of fear every time he encounters a dog (maybe not enough fear to cause him to run in terror, because some of that fear will be offset by the other belief, but there will certainly be enough fear to cause a great deal of discomfort).

The ability to "see" and consequently know that a situation is not dangerous, but at the same time find ourselves immobilized with fear, can be quite baffling if we don't understand that what we discover as the result of thinking creatively or realize from an inadvertent creative experience doesn't necessarily have enough energy to become a dominant force in our mental environment. In other words, our new awareness or discovery could very well have enough energy to act as a credible force on our perception of information, thereby causing us to perceive possibilities that would otherwise be invisible; but it might not have enough energy to act as a credible force on our behavior. In making this statement, I am operating out of the assumption that it takes more energy to act or express ourselves than the amount of energy it takes to observe something.

On the other hand, new awareness and discoveries instantly and effortlessly become dominant forces if there's nothing inside us that's in conflict with them. But if there are conflicting beliefs and we aren't willing to de-activate the conflicting forces (expending some effort), especially if they're negatively charged, then acting on what we've discovered will be a struggle at the very least, and perhaps down right impossible.

What I have just described is the psychological dilemma that virtually every trader has to resolve. Let's say you have a firm grasp of the nature of probabilities and, as a result, you "know" that the next trade is simply another trade in a series of trades that has a probable outcome. Yet you find you're still afraid to put that next trade on, or you're still susceptible to several of the fear-based trading errors we've discussed in previous chapters. Remember that the underlying cause of fear is the potential to define and interpret market information as threatening. What is the source of our potential to interpret market information as threatening? Our expectations! When the market generates information that doesn't conform to what we expect, the up and down tics seem to take on a threatening quality (become negatively charged). Consequently, we experience fear, stress, and anxiety. What is the underlying source of our expectations? Our beliefs.

In light of what you now understand about the nature of beliefs, if you are still experiencing negative states of mind when you trade, you can assume there's a conflict between what you "know" about probable outcomes and any number of other beliefs in your mental environment that are arguing (demanding expression) for something else. Keep in mind that all active beliefs demand expression, even if we don't want them to. To think in probabilities, you have to believe that every moment in the market is unique, or more specifically, that every edge has a unique outcome.

When you believe at a functional level that every edge has a unique outcome (meaning that it's a dominant belief without any other beliefs arguing for something different), you will experience a state of mind that is free of fear, stress, and anxiety when you trade. It really can't work any other way. A unique outcome is not something we have already experienced, therefore it is not something we can already know. If it were known, it could not be defined as unique. When you believe that you don't know what is going to happen next, what exactly are you expecting from the market? If you said "I don't know," you are absolutely right. If you believe that something will happen and that you don't need to know exactly what that something is to make money, then where's the potential to define and interpret market information as threatening and painful? If you said "There is none," you are absolutely right again.

Here is one more example of how beliefs demand expression. Let's look at a situation where a child's first encounter with a dog was a very positive experience. As a result, he has absolutely no problem interacting with dogs (any dog for that matter), because he has not encountered one that's unfriendly. Therefore, he has no concept (an energized belief) that it is possible for a dog to inflict any damage or cause him to experience pain.

As he learns to associate words with his memories, he will probably acquire a belief along the lines of "all dogs are friendly and fun." Therefore, every time a dog comes into his field of awareness, this belief will demand expression. From the perspective of someone who has had a negative experience with a dog, it will seem as if this child has an attitude of reckless abandon. If you tried to convince the child that he'll get bitten someday if he doesn't exercise caution, his belief will cause him to either discount or completely disregard your advice. His response would be something like "*No way!*" or "It can't happen to me."

Let's say at some point in his life he approaches an unfamiliar dog that wants to be left alone. The dog growls. The warning will go unheeded and the dog attacks the boy. From the perspective of the boy's belief system, he's just had a creative experience. What effect will this experience have on his belief that "all dogs are friendly"? Will he now be afraid of all dogs as the child in the first example was?

Unfortunately, the answers to these questions are not cut and dried, because there may be other beliefs, also demanding expression, that don't have anything specifically to do with dogs that come into play in a situation like this. For example, what if this child has a highly developed belief in betrayal (he believes he's been betrayed by some very significant people in some very significant situations that have caused him to experience intense emotional pain). If he associates the attack by this one dog as a "betrayal" by dogs in general (in essence a betrayal of his belief in dogs), then he could easily find himself afraid of all dogs. All of the positive energy contained in his original belief could instantly be transformed into negatively charged energy. The boy could justify this shift with a rationalization like "If one dog can betray me, then any dog can."

However, I do think this is an extreme and very unlikely occurrence. What is more likely is the word "all" in his original belief will instantly be de-activated and that energy will get transferred to a new belief that better reflects the true nature of dogs. This new experience caused an energy shift that forced him to learn something about the nature of dogs that he otherwise refused to consider possible. His belief in the friendliness of dogs remains intact. He will still play with dogs, but he will now exercise some discretion by consciously looking for signs of friendliness or unfriendliness.

I think that a fundamental truth about the nature of our existence is every moment in the market, as well as in everyday life, has elements of what we know (similarities) and elements that we don't or can't know because we haven't experienced it yet. Until we actively train our minds to expect a unique outcome, we will continue experiencing only what we know; everything else (other information and possibilities that are not consistent with what we know and expect) will pass us by, unperceived, discounted, distorted, outright denied, or attacked. When you truly believe that you don't need to know, you will be thinking in probabilities (the market perspective) and will have no reason to block, discount, distort, deny, or attack anything the market is offering about its potential to move in any particular direction.

If you are not experiencing the quality of mental freedom implied in that statement, and it is your desire to do so, then you must take an active role in training your mind to believe in the uniqueness of each moment, and you must de-activate any other belief that argues for something different. This process isn't any different from the one the boy in the first scenario went through, nor is it going to happen by itself. He wanted to interact with dogs without fear, but to do so he had to create a new belief and de-activate the conflicting ones. This is the secret to achieving consistent success as a trader.

3. Beliefs keep on working regardless of whether we are consciously aware of their existence in our mental environment. In other words, we don't have to actively remember or have conscious access to any particular belief for that belief to act as a force on our perception of information or on our behavior. I know it's hard to "believe" that something we can't even remember can still have an impact on our lives. But when you think about it, much of what we learn throughout our lives is stored at an unconscious or subconscious level.

If I asked you to remember each specific skill you had to learn so that you could drive a car with confidence, chances are you wouldn't remember all the things you needed to concentrate and focus on while you were in the process of learning. The first time I had the opportunity to teach a teenager how to drive, I was absolutely amazed at how much there was to learn, how much of the process I took for granted and no longer thought about at a conscious level.

Possibly the best example that illustrates this characteristic is people who drive under the influence of alcohol. On any given day or night, there are probably thousands of people who have had so much to drink that they have no idea that they have no conscious awareness of how they drove from point A to point B. It is difficult to imagine how this is possible, unless you consider that driving skills and one's belief in his ability to drive operate automatically on a much deeper level than waking consciousness.

Certainly, some percentage of these drunk drivers get into accidents, but when you compare the accident rate with the estimated number of people driving under the influence of alcohol, it's remarkable that there aren't a great many more accidents. In fact, a drunk driver is probably most likely to cause an accident when he either falls asleep or something requires a conscious decision and a fast reaction. In other words, the driving conditions are such that operating out of one's subconscious skills is not enough.

SELF-VALUATION AND TRADING

How this characteristic applies to our trading is also quite profound. The trading environment offers us an arena of unlimited opportunities to accumulate wealth. But just because the money is available and we can perceive the possibility of getting it, that doesn't necessarily mean that we (as individuals) have an unlimited sense of self-valuation. In other words, there could be a huge gap between how much money we desire for ourselves, how much we perceive is available, and how much we actually believe we are worth or deserve.

Everyone has a sense of self-valuation. The easiest way to describe this sense is to list every active belief, both conscious and subconscious, that has the potential to argue either for or against accumulating or achieving greater and greater levels of success and prosperity. Then match the energy from the positively charged beliefs against the energy from the negatively charged beliefs. If you have more positively charged energy arguing for success and prosperity than negatively charged energy arguing against them, then you have a positive sense of self-valuation. Otherwise, you have a negative sense of self-valuation.

The dynamics of how these beliefs interact with one another is not nearly so simple as I'm making it sound. In fact, it can be so complex that it could take years of sophisticated mental work to organize and sort out. What you need to know is that it's almost impossible to grow up in any social environment and not acquire some negatively charged beliefs that would argue against success or accumulating vast sums of money. Most of these self-sabotaging beliefs have long been forgotten and operate at a subconscious level, but the fact that we may have forgotten them doesn't mean they've been de-activated.

How do we acquire self-sabotaging beliefs? Unfortunately, it's extremely easy. Probably the most common way is when a child engages in some activity that a parent or teacher doesn't want him to do and the child accidently injures himself. Many parents, to get their point across to the child, will respond to a situation like this by saying, "This (whatever pain you are experiencing) wouldn't have happened to you if you didn't deserve it," or "You disobeyed me and look what happened, God punished you." The problem with making or hearing statements like this is that there's a potential for the child to associate every future injury with these same statements and, subsequently, form a belief that he must be an unworthy person, undeserving of success, happiness, or love.

Anything we feel guilty about can have an adverse effect on our sense of self-worth. Usually guilt is associated with being a bad person, and most people believe that bad people should be punished, certainly not rewarded. Some religions teach children that having a lot of money isn't godly or spiritual. Some people believe that making money in certain ways is wrong, even though it may be perfectly legal and moral from society's perspective. Again, you may not have a specific recollection of learning something that would argue against the success you perceive as possible, but that doesn't mean that what you learned is no longer having an effect.

The way these subconscious self-sabotaging beliefs manifest themselves in our trading is usually in the form of lapses in focus or concentration, resulting in any number of trading errors, like putting in a buy for a sell or vice versa, or allowing yourself to give in to distracting thoughts that compel you to leave the screen, only to find out when you return that you missed the big trade of the day. I've worked with many traders who achieved various levels of consistent success, but found they just couldn't break through certain thresholds in acquiring equity. They discovered an invisible but very real barrier similar to the proverbial glass ceiling that many women executives experience in the corporate world.

Every time these traders hit the barrier, they experienced a significant draw down, regardless of the market conditions. However, when asked about what happened, they typically blamed their sudden run of bad luck on just that—luck or the vagaries of the market. Interestingly, they typically created a steadily rising equity curve, sometimes over a period of several months, and the significant draw down always occurred at the same spot in their equity curve. I describe this psychological phenomenon as being in a "negative zone." As magically as money can flow into a trader's accounts when he is "in the zone," it can just as easily flow out, if he is in a negative zone where unresolved self-valuation issues mysteriously act on his perception of information and behavior.

I am not implying here that you have to de-activate every belief that would argue against your ever-expanding positive sense of self-valuation, because you don't. But you must be aware of the presence of such beliefs, and take specific steps in your trading regimen to compensate when they start expressing themselves.

CHAPTER 11

THINKING LIKE
A TRADER

If you asked me to distill trading down to its simplest form, I would say that it is a pattern recognition numbers game. We use market analysis to identify the patterns, define the risk, and determine when to take profits. The trade either works or it doesn't. In any case, we go on to the next trade. It's that simple, but it's certainly not easy. In fact, trading is probably the hardest thing you'll ever attempt to be successful at. That's not because it requires intellect; quite the contrary! But because the more you think you know, the less successful you'll be. Trading is hard because you have to operate in a state of not having to know, even though your analysis may turn out at times to be "perfectly" correct. To operate in a state of not having to know, you have to properly manage your expectations. To properly manage your expectations, you must realign your mental environment so that you believe without a shadow of a doubt in the five fundamental truths.

In this chapter, I am going to give you a trading exercise that will integrate these truths about the market at a functional level in your mental environment. In the process, I'll take you through the three stages of development of a trader.

The first stage is the *mechanical* stage. In this stage, you:

1. Build the self-trust necessary to operate in an unlimited environment.

2. Learn to flawlessly execute a trading system.

3. Train your mind to think in probabilities (the five fundamental truths).

4. Create a strong, unshakeable belief in your consistency as a trader.

Once you have completed this first stage, you can then advance to the *subjective* stage of trading. In this stage, you use anything you have ever learned about the nature of market movement to do whatever it is you want to do. There's a lot of freedom in this stage, so you will have to learn how to monitor your susceptibility to make the kind of trading errors that are the result of any unresolved self-valuation issues I referred to in the last chapter.

The third stage is the *intuitive* stage. Trading intuitively is the most advanced stage of development. It is the trading equivalent of earning a black belt in the martial arts. The difference is that you can't try to be intuitive, because intuition is spontaneous. It doesn't come from what we know at a rational level. The rational part of our mind seems to be inherently mistrustful of information received from a source that it doesn't understand. Sensing that something is about to happen is a form of knowing that is very different from anything we know rationally. I've worked with many traders who frequently had a very strong intuitive sense of what was going to happen next, only to be confronted with the rational part of themselves that consistently, argued for another course of action. Of course, if they had followed their intuition, they would have experienced a very satisfying outcome. Instead, what they ended up with was usually very unsatisfactory, especially when compared with what they otherwise perceived as possible. The only way I know of that you can try to be intuitive is to work at setting up a state of mind most conducive to receiving and acting on your intuitive impulses.

THE MECHANICAL STAGE

The mechanical stage of trading is specifically designed to build the kind of trading skills (trust, confidence, and thinking in probabilities) that will virtually compel you to create consistent results. I define consistent results as a steadily rising equity curve with only minor draw downs that are the natural consequence of edges that didn't work.

Other than finding a pattern that puts the odds of a winning trade in your favor, achieving a steadily rising equity curve is a function of systematically eliminating any susceptibility you may have to making the kind of fear, euphoric or self-valuation based trading errors I have described throughout this book. Eliminating the errors and expanding your sense of self-valuation will require the acquisition of skills that are all psychological in nature.

The skills are psychological because each one, in its purest form, is simply a belief. Remember that the beliefs we operate out of will determine our state of mind and shape our experiences in ways that constantly reinforce what we already believe to be true. How truthful a belief is (relative to the environmental conditions) can be determined by how well it serves us; that is, the degree to which it helps us satisfy our objectives. If producing consistent results is your primary objective as a trader, then creating a belief (a conscious, energized concept that resists change and demands expression) that *"I am a consistently successful trader"* will act as a primary source of energy that will manage your perceptions, interpretations, expectations, and actions in ways that satisfy the belief and, consequently, the objective.

Creating a dominant belief that "I am a consistently successful trader" requires adherence to several principles of consistent success. Some of these principles will undoubtedly be in direct conflict with some of the beliefs you've already acquired about trading. If this is the case, then what you have is a classic example of beliefs that are in direct conflict with desire.

The energy dynamic here is no different from what it was for the boy who wanted to be like the other children who were not afraid to play with dogs. He desired to express himself in a way that he found, at least initially, virtually impossible. To satisfy his desire, he had to step into an active process of transformation. His technique was simple: He tried as hard as he could to stay focused on what he was trying to accomplish and, little by little, he de-activated the conflicting belief and strengthened the belief that was consistent with his desire.

At some point, if that is your desire, then you will have to step into the process of transforming yourself into a consistent winner. When it comes to personal transformation, the most important ingredients are your willingness to change, the clarity of your intent, and the strength of your desire. Ultimately, for this process to work, you must choose consistency over every other reason or justification you have for trading. If all of these ingredients are sufficiently present, then regardless of the internal obstacles you find yourself up against, what you desire will eventually prevail.

Observe Yourself

The first step in the process of creating consistency is to start noticing what you're thinking, saying, and doing. Why? Because everything we think, say, or do as a trader contributes to and, therefore, reinforces some belief in our mental system. Because the process of becoming consistent is psychological in nature, it shouldn't come as a surprise that you'll have to start paying attention to your various psychological processes.

The idea is eventually to learn to become an objective observer of your own thoughts, words, and deeds. Your first line of defense against committing a trading error is to catch yourself thinking about it. Of course, the last line of defense is to catch yourself in the act. If you don't commit yourself to becoming an observer to these processes, your realizations will always come after the experience, usually when you are in a state of deep regret and frustration.

Observing yourself objectively implies doing it without judgment or any harsh criticism as a consequence for what you're noticing about yourself. This might not be so easy for some of you to do considering the harsh, judgmental treatment you may have received from other people throughout your life. As a result, one quickly learns to associate any mistake with emotional pain. No one likes to be in a state of emotional pain, so we typically avoid acknowledging what we have learned to define as a mistake for as long as possible. Not confronting mistakes in our everyday lives usually doesn't have the same disastrous consequences it can have if we avoid confronting our mistakes as traders.

For example, when I am working with floor traders, the analogy I use to illustrate how precarious a situation they are in is to ask them to imagine themselves walking across a bridge over the Grand Canyon. The width of the bridge is directly related to the number of contracts they trade. So, for example, for a one-contract trader the bridge is very wide, say 20 feet. A bridge 20 feet wide allows you a great deal of tolerance for error, so you don't have to be inordinately careful or focused on each step you take. Still, if you do happen to stumble and trip over the edge, the drop to the canyon floor is one mile.

I don't know how many people would walk across a narrow bridge with no guardrails, where the ground is a mile down, but my guess is relatively few. Similarly, few people will take the kinds of risks associated with trading on the floor of the futures exchanges. Certainly a one-contract floor trader can do a great deal of damage to himself, not unlike falling off a mile-high bridge. But a one-contract trader also can give himself a wide tolerance for errors, miscalculations, or unusually violent market moves where he could find himself on the wrong side.

On the other hand, one of the biggest floor traders I ever worked with trades for his own account with an average position of 500 Treasury bond futures at a time. He often puts on a position of well over a thousand contracts. A position of 1,000 T-bond contracts amounts to $31,500 per tic (the smallest incremental price change that a bond contract can make). Of course, T-bond futures can be very volatile and can trade several tics in either direction in a matter of seconds.

As the size of a trader's position increases, the width of our bridge over the Grand Canyon narrows. In the case of the large bond trader, the bridge has narrowed to the size of a thin wire. Obviously, he has to be extremely well-balanced and very focused on each step that he takes. The slightest misstep or gust of wind could cause him to fall off the wire. Next stop, one mile down.

Now, when he's in the trading pit, that tiny misstep or slight gust of wind is the equivalent to one distracting thought. That's all, just a thought or anything else where he allows himself to lose his focus for even a second or two. In that moment of distraction, he could miss his last favorable opportunity to liquidate his position. The next price level with enough volume to take him out of his trade could be several tics away, either creating a huge loss or forcing him to give a substantial winning trade back to the market.

If producing consistent results is a function of eliminating errors, then it is an understatement to say that you will encounter great difficulty in achieving your objective if you can't acknowledge a mistake. Obviously, this is something very few people can do, and it accounts for why there are so few consistent winners. In fact, the tendency not to acknowledge a mistake is so pervasive throughout mankind, it could lead one to assume that it's an inherent characteristic of human nature. I do not believe this is the case, nor do I believe we are born with the capacity to ridicule or think less of ourselves for making a mistake, miscalculation, or error.

Making mistakes is a natural function of living and will continue to be until we reach a point at which:

1. all our beliefs are in absolute harmony with our desires, and

2. all our beliefs are structured in such a way that they are completely consistent with what works from the environment's perspective.

Obviously, if our beliefs are not consistent with what works from the environment's perspective, the potential for making a mistake is high, if not inevitable. We won't be able to perceive the appropriate set of steps to our objective. Worse, we won't be able to perceive that what we want may not be available, or available in the quantity we desire or at the time when we want it.

On the other hand, mistakes that are the result of beliefs that are in conflict with our objectives aren't always apparent or obvious. We know they will act as opposing forces, expressing their versions of the truth on our consciousness, and they can do that in many ways. The most difficult to detect is a distracting thought that causes a momentary lapse in focus or concentration. On the surface this may not sound significant. But, as in the analogy of the bridge over the canyon, when there's a lot at stake, even a slightly diminished capacity to stay focused can result in an error of disastrous proportions. This principle applies whether it's trading, sporting events, or computer programming. When our intent is clear and undiminished by any opposing energy, then our capacity to stay focused is greater, and the more likely it is that we will accomplish our objective.

Earlier I defined a winning attitude as a positive expectation of our efforts, with an acceptance that whatever results we do get are a perfect reflection of our level of development and what we need to learn to do better. What separates the "consistently great" athletes and performers from everyone else is their distinct lack of fear of making a mistake. The reason they aren't afraid is that they don't have a reason to think less of themselves when they do make a mistake, meaning they don't have a reservoir of negatively charged energy waiting to well up and pounce on their conscious thought process like a lion waiting for the right moment to pounce on its intended prey. What accounts for this uncommon capacity to quickly move beyond their errors without criticizing themselves? One explanation may be that they grew up with extremely unusual parents, teachers, and coaches, who by their words and examples taught them to correct their miscalculations and errors with genuine love, affection, and acceptance. I say "extremely unusual" because many of us grew up with just the opposite experience. We were taught to correct our mistakes or miscalculations with anger, impatience, and a distinct lack of acceptance. Is it possible that, for the great athletes, their past posi-tive experiences with respect to mistakes caused them to acquire a belief that mistakes simply point the way to where they need to focus their efforts to grow and improve themselves?

With a belief like that, there's no source of negatively charged energy and consequently no source for self-denigrating thoughts. However, the rest of us, who did grow up experiencing a plethora of negative reactions to our actions, would naturally acquire beliefs about mistakes: "Mistakes must be avoided at all costs," "There must be something wrong with me if I make a mistake," "I must be a screw-up," or "I must be a bad person if I make a mistake."

Remember that every thought, word, and deed reinforces some belief we have about ourselves. If, by repeated negative self-criticism, we acquire a belief that we're "screw-ups," that belief will find a way to express itself in our thoughts, causing us to become distracted and to screw up; on our words, causing us to say things about ourselves or about others (if we notice the same characteristics in them) that reflect our belief; and on our actions, causing us to behave in ways that are overtly self-sabotaging.

If you're going to become a consistent winner, mistakes can't exist in the kind of negatively charged context in which they are held by most people. You have to be able to monitor yourself to some degree, and that will be difficult to do if you have the potential to experience emotional pain if and when you find yourself in the process of making an error. If this potential exists, you have two choices:

1. You can work on acquiring a new set of positively charged beliefs about what it means to make a mistake, along with de-activat-ing any negatively charged beliefs that would argue otherwise or cause you to think less of yourself for making a mistake.

2. If you find this first choice undesirable, you can compensate for the potential to make errors by the way you set up your trading regime. This means that if you're going to trade and not monitor yourself, but at the same time you desire consistent results, then trad-ing exclusively from the mechanical stage will resolve the dilemma.

Otherwise, learning how to monitor yourself is a relatively simple process once you have rid yourself of negatively charged energy associated with mistakes. In fact, it's easy. All you have to do is decide why you want to monitor yourself, which means you first need to have a clear purpose in mind. When you're clear about your purpose, simply start directing your attention to what you think, say, or do.

If and when you notice that you're not focused on your objective or on the incremental steps to accomplish your objective, choose to redirect your thoughts, words, or actions in a way that is consistent with what you are trying to accomplish. Keep redirecting as often as necessary. The more willfully you engage in this process, especially if you can do it with some degree of conviction, the faster you will create a mental framework free to function in a way that is consistent with your objectives, without any resistance from conflicting beliefs.

THE ROLE OF SELF-DISCIPLINE

I call the process I just described *self-discipline*. I define self-discipline as a mental technique to redirect (as best we can) our focus of attention to the object of our goal or desire, when that goal or desire conflicts with some other component (belief) of our mental environment.

The first thing you should notice about this definition is that self-discipline is a technique to create a new mental framework. It is not a personality trait; people aren't born with self-discipline. In fact, when you consider how I define it, being born with discipline isn't even possible. However, as a technique to be used in the process of personal transformation, anybody can choose to use self-discipline.

Here is an example from my life that illustrates the underlying dynamics of how this technique works. In 1978 I decided that I wanted to become a runner. I don't exactly remember what my underlying motivation was, except that I had spent the previous eight years in a very inactive life style. I wasn't involved with any sports or hobbies, unless you call watching television a hobby.

Previously in both high school and at least part of college I was very active in sports, especially ice hockey. However, coming out of college, my life was unfolding in the way that was very different from what I had expected. It was not to my liking, but at the time I felt powerless to do anything about it. This led to a period of inactivity, which is a nice way of saying that I was severely depressed.

Again, I'm not sure what prompted me to suddenly want to become a runner (maybe I saw some TV program that sparked my interest). I do, however, remember that the motivation was very strong. So, I went out and bought myself some running shoes, put them on, and went out to run. The first thing I discovered was that I couldn't do it. I didn't have the physical stamina to run more than fifty or sixty yards. This was very surprising. I didn't realize, nor would I have ever believed, that I was so out of shape that I couldn't run even a hundred yards. This realization was so disheartening that I didn't attempt to run again for two or three weeks. The next time out, I still couldn't run more than fifty or sixty yards. I tried again the next day with, of course, the same result. I became so discouraged about my deteriorated physical condition that I didn't run again for another four months.

Now, it's the spring of 1979. I'm once again determined to become a runner, but, at the same time, very frustrated with my lack of progress. As I was contemplating my dilemma, it occurred to me that one of my problems was that I didn't have a goal to work towards. Saying that I wanted to be a runner was great, but what did that mean? I really didn't know; it was too vague and abstract. I had to have something more tangible to work towards. So I decided that I wanted to be able to run five miles by the end of the summer.

Five miles seemed insurmountable at the time, but thinking that I might be able to do it generated a lot of enthusiasm. This increased level of enthusiasm gave me enough impetus to run four times that week. At the end of this first week, I was really surprised to discover even a little bit of exercise improved my stamina and ability to run a little farther each time. This created even more enthusiasm, so I went out and bought a stop watch and blank book to be used as a running diary. I set up a two-mile course, and marked off each quarter mile. In the diary I entered the date, my distance, my time, and how I felt physically each time I ran.

Now I thought I was well on my way to the five miles, until I literally ran into my next set of problems. The biggest were the conflicting and distracting thoughts that flooded my consciousness every time I decided I wanted to go out and run. I was amazed at the number (and intensity) of the reasons I found for not doing it: "It's hot [or] cold outside," "It looks like it's going to rain," "I'm still a little tired from the last time I ran (even though it was three days ago)," "Nobody else I know is doing this," or the most prevalent, "I'll go as soon as this TV program is over" (of course I never went).

I didn't know of any other way to deal with this conflicting mental energy except to redirect my conscious attention toward what I was trying to accomplish. I really wanted to get to five miles by the end of the summer. I found that *sometimes* my desire was stronger than the conflict. As a result, I managed to get my running shoes on, actually step outside, and start running. However, more times than not, my conflicting and distracting thoughts caused me to stay put. In fact, in the beginning stages, I estimate that two-thirds of the time I was unable to get past the conflicting energy.

The next problem I encountered was that when I started approaching the point where I was able to run one mile, I was so thrilled with myself that it occurred to me I was going to need an additional mechanism to get me to the five miles. I reasoned that once I got to the point where I could run two or maybe three miles, I would be so overwhelmingly pleased with myself that I wouldn't feel any need to fulfill my five-mile objective. So I made a rule for myself. You could call it the five-mile rule. "If I managed to get my running shoes on and get outside in spite of all the conflicting thoughts trying to talk me out of it, I committed myself to running at least one step farther than the last time I ran." It was certainly all right if I ran more than one step further, but it couldn't be less than one step, no matter what. As it turns out, I never broke this rule, and by the end of the summer, I made it to five miles.

But then, something really interesting and completely unanticipated happened before I got there. As I got closer to fulfilling my
five-mile objective, little by little, the conflicting thoughts began to
dissipate. Eventually they didn't exist at all. At that point, I found that
if I wanted to run, I was completely free to do so without any mental
resistance, conflict, or competing thoughts. Given what a struggle it
had been, I was amazed (to say the least). The result: I went on to run
on a very regular basis for the next 16 years.

For those of you who may be interested, I don't run so much
now because five years ago I decided to start playing ice hockey
again. Hockey is an extremely strenuous sport. Sometimes I play as
many as four times a week. Considering my age (over 50) and the
level of exertion the sport requires, it usually takes me a day or two
to recover, which doesn't leave much room for running any more.

Now, if you take these experiences and put them into the context of what we now understand about the nature of beliefs, there are
a number of observations we can make:

1. Initially, my desire to be a runner had no foundation of support in my mental system. In other words, there was no other source
of energy (an energized concept demanding expression) consistent
with my desire.

2. I actually had to do something to create that support. To create a belief that "I am a runner" required that I create a series of experiences consistent with the new belief. Remember that everything we
think, say, or do contributes energy to some belief in our mental system. Each time I experienced a conflicting thought and was able to
successfully refocus on my objective, with enough conviction to get
me into my running shoes and out the door, I added energy to the
belief that "I am a runner." And, just as important, I inadvertently
drew energy away from all of the beliefs that would argue otherwise.
I say inadvertently because there are various techniques specifically
designed to identify and de-activate conflicting beliefs, but at that
time in my life, I didn't understand the underlying dynamics of the

process of transformation I was going through. So, it wouldn't have occurred to me to avail myself of such techniques.

3. Now I can effortlessly (from a mental perspective) express myself as a runner, because "I am a runner." That energized concept is now a functioning part of my identity. When I first started out, I happened to have a number of conflicting beliefs about running. As a result, I needed the technique of self-discipline to become one. Now I don't need self-discipline because "being a runner" is "who I am." When our beliefs are completely aligned with our goals or desires, there's no source of conflicting energy. If there's no source of conflicting energy, then there's no source of distracting thoughts, excuses, rationalizations, justifications, or mistakes (conscious or subconscious).

4. Beliefs can be changed, and if it's possible to change one belief, then it's possible to change any belief, if you understand that you really aren't changing them, but are only transferring energy from one concept to another. (The form of the belief targeted for change remains intact.) Therefore, two completely contradictory beliefs can exist in your mental system, side by side. But if you've drawn the energy out of one belief and completely energized the other, no contradiction exists from a functional perspective; only the belief combined with the energy will have the capacity to act as a force on your state of mind, on your perception and interpretation of information, and your behavior.

Now, the sole purpose of trading mechanically is to transform yourself into a consistently successful trader. If there's anything in your mental environment that's in conflict with the principles of creating the belief that "*I am a consistently successful trader*," then you will need to employ the technique of self-discipline to integrate these principles as a dominant, functioning part of your identity. Once the principles become "who you are," you will no longer need self-discipline, because the process of "being consistent" will become effortless.

Remember that consistency is not the same as the ability to put on a winning trade, or even a string of winning trades for that matter, because putting on a winning trade requires absolutely no skill. All you have to do is guess correctly, which is no different than guessing the outcome of a coin toss, whereas consistency is a state of mind that, once achieved, won't allow you to "be" any other way. You won't have to try to be consistent because it will be a natural function of your identity. In fact, if you have to try, it's an indication that you haven't completely integrated the principles of consistent success as dominant, unconflicted beliefs.

For example, predefining your risk is a step in the process of "being consistent." If it takes any special effort to predefine your risk, if you have to consciously remind yourself to do it, if you experience any conflicting thoughts (in essence, trying to talk you out of doing it), or if you find yourself in a trade where you haven't predefined your risk, then this principle is not a dominant, functioning part of your identity. It isn't "who you are." If it were, it wouldn't even occur to you not to predefine your risk.

If and when all of the sources of conflict have been de-activated, there's no longer a potential for you to "be" any other way. What was once a struggle will become virtually effortless. At that point, it may seem to other people that you are so disciplined (because you can do something they find difficult, if not impossible), but the reality is that you aren't being disciplined at all; you are simply functioning from a different set of beliefs that compel you to behave in a way that is consistent with your desires, goals, or objectives.

CREATING A BELIEF IN CONSISTENCY

Creating a belief that *"I am a consistent winner"* is the primary objective, but like my intention to become a runner, it's too broad and abstract to implement without breaking it down into a step-by-step process. So what I'm going to do is break this belief down into its smallest definable parts and then give you a plan to integrate each part as a dominant belief. The following sub-beliefs are the building

blocks that provide the underlying structure for what it me
a consistent winner."

I AM A CONSISTENT WINNER BECAUSE:

1. **I objectively identify my edges.**
2. **I predefine the risk of every trade.**
3. **I completely accept the risk or I am willing to let go of the trade.**
4. **I act on my edges without reservation or hesitation.**
5. **I pay myself as the market makes money available to me.**
6. **I continually monitor my susceptibility for making errors.**
7. **I understand the absolute necessity of these principles of consistent success and, therefore, I never violate them.**

These beliefs are the seven principles of consistency. To integrate these principles into your mental system at a functional level requires that you purposely create a series of experiences that are consistent with them. This is no different from the boy who wanted to play with dogs or my desire to be a runner. Before he could play with a dog, the boy first had to make several attempts just to get close to one. Eventually, as the balance of energy in his mental system shifted, he could play with dogs without any internal resistance. To become a runner, I had to create the experience of running in spite of everything inside me that argued otherwise. Eventually, as the energy shifted more and more in favor of this new definition of myself, running became a natural expression of my identity.

Obviously, what we're trying to accomplish here is far more complex than becoming a runner or petting a dog, but the underlying dynamics of the process are identical. We'll start with a specific objective. The first principle of consistency is the belief, "I objectively identify my edges." The key word here is *objectively*. Being objective means there's no potential to define, interpret, and therefore perceive any market information from either a painful or euphoric perspective. The way to be objective is to operate out of beliefs that keep your expectations neutral and to always take the unknown forces into consideration.

Remember, you have to specifically train your mind to be objective and to stay focused in the "now moment opportunity flow." Our minds are not naturally wired to think this way, so to be an objective observer you have to learn to think from the market's perspective. From the market's perspective, there are always unknown forces (traders) waiting to act on price movement. Therefore, from the market's perspective, "every moment is truly unique," even though the moment may look, sound, or feel exactly the same as some moment logged away in your memory bank.

The instant you either decide or assume you know what's going to happen next, you will automatically expect to be right. However, what you know, at least at the rational level of thinking, can only take into consideration your unique past, which may not have any relationship to what is actually happening from the market's perspective. At that point, any market information that is not consistent with your expectation has the potential to be defined and interpreted as painful. To avoid experiencing the pain, your mind will automatically compensate, with both conscious and subconscious pain-avoidance mechanisms, for any differences between what you expect and what the market is offering.

What you will experience is commonly referred to as an "illusion." In a state of illusion, you are neither objective nor connected to the "now moment opportunity flow." Instead, you become susceptible to committing all the typical trading errors (hesitating, jumping the gun, not predefining your risk, defining your risk but refusing to take the loss and letting the trade turn into a bigger loser, getting out of a winning trade too soon, not taking any profits out of a winning trade, letting a winning trade turn into a loser, moving a stop closer to your entry point, getting stopped out and watching the market trade back in your favor, or trading too large a position in relationship to your equity). The five fundamental truths about the market will keep your expectations neutral, focus your mind in the "now moment opportunity flow" (by disassociating the present moment from your past), and, therefore, eliminate your potential to commit these errors.

When you stop making trading errors, you'll begin trusting yourself. As your sense of self-trust increases, so will your sense of self-confidence. The greater your confidence, the easier it will be to execute your trades (act on your edges without reservation or hesitation). The five truths will also create a state of mind in which you will genuinely accept the risks of trading. When you genuinely accept the risks, you will be at peace with any outcome. When you're at peace with any outcome, you will experience a carefree, objective state of mind, where you make yourself available to perceive and act upon whatever the market is offering you (from its perspective) at any given "now moment."

The first objective is to integrate as a dominant belief, "I objectively identify my edges." The challenge now is, how do you get there? How do you transform yourself into a person who can consistently think in the market's perspective?

The process of transformation starts with your desire and your willingness to refocus on the object of your desire (self-discipline). Desire is a force. It does not have to coincide or agree with anything that you currently believe to be true about the nature of trading. A clear desire aimed squarely at a specific objective is a very powerful tool. You can use the force of your desire to create an entirely new version or dimension to your identity; shift energy between two or more conflicting concepts; or change the context or polarity of your memories from negative to positive.

I'm sure you are familiar with the saying, "Make up your mind." The implication of "making up our minds" is that we decide exactly what we desire with so much clarity (absolutely no lingering doubts) and with so much conviction that literally nothing stands in our way, either internally or externally. If there's enough force behind our resolve, it's possible to experience a major shift in our mental structure virtually instantaneously. De-activating internal conflicts is not a function of time; it's a function-focused desire (although it can take a considerable amount of time to get to the point where we really make up our minds). Otherwise, in the absence of extreme clarity and conviction, the technique of self-discipline, over time, will do the job quite nicely (if, of course, you're willing to use it).

To get there, you must "make up your mind," with as much conviction and clarity as possible, that more than anything else you desire consistency (the state of mind of trust, confidence, and objectivity) from your trading. This is necessary because if you're like most traders, you're going to be up against some very formidable conflicting forces. For example, if you've been trading to get high from the euphoria of catching a big move, to impress your family and friends, to be a hero, to fulfill an addiction to random rewards, to be right about your predictions, or for any other reason that has nothing to do with being consistent, then you'll find the force of these other motivations will not only act as an obstacle making the trading exercise I'm about to give you very difficult, but it could very well be strong enough even to keep you from doing the exercise at all.

Remember the boy who had no desire to be like the other children and interact with dogs? In essence, he decided to live with the active contradiction between his minimally charged positive belief that not all dogs are dangerous and his core, negatively charged belief that all dogs are dangerous. He had the ability to perceive friendly dogs, but at the same time found it impossible to interact with them. Unless he desires to change it, the imbalance of energy between these two beliefs will stay exactly as it is for his entire life.

To even start this process, you have to want consistency so much that you would be willing to give up all the other reasons, motivations, or agendas you have for trading that aren't consistent with the process of integrating the beliefs that create consistency. A clear, intense desire is an absolute prerequisite if you're going to make this process work for you.

EXERCISE

LEARNING TO TRADE AN EDGE
LIKE A CASINO

The object of this exercise is to convince yourself that trading is just a simple game of probabilities (numbers), not much different from pulling the handle of a slot machine. At the micro level, the outcomes to individual edges are independent occurrences and random in relationship to one another. At the macro level, the outcomes over a series of trades will produce consistent results.

From a probabilities perspective, this means that instead of being the person playing the slot machine, as a trader, you can be the casino, if:

1. you have an edge that genuinely puts the odds of success in your favor;

2. you can think about trading in the appropriate manner (the five fundamental truths); and

3. you can do everything you need to do over a series of trades.

Then, like the casinos, you will own the game and be a consistent winner.

SETTING UP THE EXERCISE

Pick a market. Choose one actively traded stock or futures contract to trade. It doesn't matter what it is, as long as it's liquid and you can afford the margin requirements for trading at least three hundred shares or three futures contracts per trade.

Choose a set of market variables that define an edge. This can be any trading system you want. The trading system or methodology you choose can be mathematical, mechanical, or visual (based on patterns in price charts). It doesn't matter whether you personally design the system or purchase it from someone else, nor do you need to take a long time or be too picky trying to find or develop the best or right system. This exercise is not about system development and it is not a test of your analytical abilities.

In fact, the variables you choose can even be considered mediocre by most traders' standards, because what you are going to learn from doing this exercise is not dependent upon whether you actually make money. If you consider this exercise an educational expense, it will cut down on the amount of time and effort you might otherwise expend trying to find the most profitable edges.

For those of you who might be wondering, I'm not going to make any specific recommendations about what system or variables you should use, because I assume that most of the people reading this book are already well schooled in technical analysis. If you need additional assistance, there are hundreds of books available on the topic, as well as system vendors who are more than willing to sell you their ideas. However, if you've made a genuine attempt to do this on your own but are still having problems picking a system, you can contact me at *markdouglas.com* or *tradinginthezone.com* and I will make some recommendations.

Whatever system you choose to use has to fit within the following specifications.

Trade Entry. The variables you use to define your edge have to be absolutely precise. The system has to be designed so that it does not require you to make any subjective decisions or judgments about whether your edge is present. If the market is aligned in a way that conforms with the rigid variables of your system, then you have a trade; if not, then you don't have a trade. Period! No other extraneous or random factors can enter into the equation.

Stop-Loss Exit. The same conditions apply to getting out of a trade that's not working. Your methodology has to tell you *exactly* how much you need to risk to find out if the trade is going to work. There is always an optimum point at which the possibility of a trade not working is so diminished, especially in relationship to the profit potential, that you're better off taking your loss and getting your mind clear to act on the next edge. Let the market structure determine where this optimum point is, rather than using an arbitrary dollar amount that you are willing to risk on a trade.

In any case, whatever system you choose, it has to be absolutely exact, requiring no subjective decision making. Again, no extraneous or random variables can enter into the equation.

Time Frame. Your trading methodology can be in any time frame that suits you, but all your entry and exit signals have to be based in the same time frame. For example, if you use variables that identify a particular support and resistance pattern on a 30-minute bar chart, then your risk and profit objective calculations also have to be determined in a 30-minute time frame.

However, trading in one time frame does not preclude you from using other time frames as filters. For example, you could have as a filter a rule that states you're only going to take trades that are in the direction of the major trend. There's an old trading axiom that "The trend is your friend." It means that you have a higher probability of success when you trade in the direction of the major trend, if there is one. In fact, the lowest-risk trade, with the highest probability of success, occurs when you are buying dips (support) in an up-trending market or selling rallies (resistance) in a down-trending market.

To illustrate how this rule works, let's say that you've chosen a precise way of identifying support and resistance patterns in a 30-minute time frame as your edge. The rule is that you are only going to take trades in the direction of the major trend. A trending market is defined as a series of higher highs and higher lows for an up-trending market and a series of lower highs and lower lows for a down-trending market. The longer the time frame, the more significant the trend, so a trending market on a daily bar chart is more significant than a trending market on a 30-minute bar chart. Therefore, the trend on the daily bar chart would take precedence over the trend on the 30-minute bar chart and would be considered the major trend.

To determine the direction of the major trend, look at what is happening on a daily bar chart. If the trend is up on the daily, you are only going to look for a sell-off or retracement down to what your edge defines as support on the 30-minute chart. That's where you will become a buyer. On the other hand, if the trend is down on the daily, you are only going to look for a rally up to what your edge defines as a resistance level to be a seller on the 30-minute chart.

Your objective is to determine, in a down-trending market, how far it can rally on an intraday basis and still not violate the symmetry of the longer trend. In an up-trending market, your objective is to determine how far it can sell off on an intraday basis without violating the symmetry of the longer trend. There's usually very little risk associated with these intraday support and resistance points, because you don't have to let the market go very far beyond them to tell you the trade isn't working.

Taking Profits. Believe it or not, of all the skills one needs to learn to be a consistently successful trader, learning to take profits is probably the most difficult to master. A multitude of personal, often very complicated psychological factors, as well as the effectiveness of one's market analysis, enter into the equation. Unfortunately, sorting out this complex matrix of issues goes way beyond the scope of this book. I point this out so that those of you who might be inclined to beat yourselves up for leaving money on the table can relax and give yourselves a break. Even after you've acquired all the other skills, it might take a very long time before you get this one down pat.

Don't despair. There is a way to set up a profit-taking regime that at least fulfills the objective of the fifth principle of consistency ("I pay myself as the market makes money available to me"). If you're going to establish a belief in yourself that you're a consistent winner, then you will have to create experiences that correspond with that belief. Because the object of the belief is winning consistently, how you take profits in a winning trade is of paramount importance.

This is the only part of the exercise in which you will have some degree of discretion about what you do. The underlying premise is that, in a winning trade, you never know how far the market is going to go in your direction. Markets rarely go straight up or straight down. (Many of the NASDAQ Internet stocks in the fall of 1999 were an obvious exception to this statement.) Typically, markets go up and then retrace some portion of the upward move; or go down and then retrace some portion of the downward move.

These proportional retracements can make it very difficult to stay in a winning trade. You would have to be an extremely sophisticated and objective analyst to make the distinction between a normal retracement, when the market still has the potential to move in the original direction of your trade, and a retracement that isn't normal, when the potential for any further movement in the original direction of your trade is greatly diminished, if not nonexistent.

If you never know how far the market is going to go in your direction, then when and how do you take profits? The question of when is a function of your ability to read the market and pick the most likely spots for it to stop. In the absence of an ability to do this objectively, the best course of action from a psychological perspective is to divide your position into thirds (or quarters), and scale out the position as the market moves in your favor. If you are trading futures contracts, this means your minimum position for a trade is at least three (or four) contracts. For stocks, the minimum position is any number of shares that is divisible by three (or four), so you don't end up with an odd-lot order.

Here's the way I scale out of a winning position. When I first started trading, especially during the first three years (1979 through 1981), I would thoroughly and regularly analyze the results of my trading activities. One of the things I discovered was that I rarely got stopped out of a trade for a loss, without the market first going at least a little way in my direction. On average, only one out of every ten trades was an immediate loser that never went in my direction. Out of the other 25 to 30 percent of the trades that were ultimately losers, the market usually went in my direction by three or four tics before revising and stopping me out. I calculated that if I got into the habit of taking at least a third of my original position off every time the market gave me those three or four tics, at the end of the year the accumulated winnings would go a long way towards paying my expenses. I was right. To this day, I always, without reservation or hesitation, take off a portion of a winning position whenever the market gives me a little to take. How much that might be depends on the market; it will be a different amount in each case. For example, in Treasury bond futures, I take a third of my position off when I get four tics. In the S&P futures, I take a third off for a profit of one and a half to two full points.

In a bond trade, I usually don't risk more than six tics to find out if the trade is going to work. Using a three-contract trade as an example, here's how it works: If I get into a position and the market immediately goes against me without giving me at least four tics first, I get stopped out of the trade for an 18-tic loss, but as I've indicated, this doesn't happen often. More likely, the trade goes in my favor by some small amount before becoming a loser. If it goes in my favor by at least four tics, I take those four tics on one contract. What I have done is reduce my total risk on the other two contracts by 10 tics. If the market then stops me out of the last two contracts, the net loss on the trade is only 8 tics.

If I don't get stopped out on the last two contracts and the market moves in my direction, I take the next third of the position off at some predetermined profit objective. This is based on some longer time frame support or resistance, or on the test of a previous significant high or low. When I take profits on the second third, I also move the stop-loss to my original entry point. Now I have a net profit on the trade regardless of what happens to the last third of the position.

In other words, I now have a "risk-free opportunity." I can't emphasize enough nor can the publisher make the words on this page big enough to stress how important it is for you to experience the state of "risk-free opportunity." When you set up a situation in which there is "risk-free opportunity," there's no way to lose unless something extremely unusual happens, like a limit up or limit down move through your stop. If, under normal circumstances, there's no way to lose, you get to experience what it really feels like to be in a trade with a relaxed, carefree state of mind.

To illustrate this point, imagine that you are in a winning trade; the market made a fairly significant move in your direction, but you didn't take any profits because you thought it was going even further. However, instead of going further, the market trades all the way back to or very close to your original entry point. You panic and, as a result, liquidate the trade, because you don't want to let what was once a winning trade turn into a loser. But as soon as you're out, the market bounces right back into what would have been a winning trade. If you had locked in some profits by scaling out, putting yourself in a risk-free opportunity situation, it's very unlikely that you would have panicked or felt any stress or anxiety for that matter.

I still have a third of my position left. What now? I look for the most likely place for the market to stop. This is usually a significant high or low in a longer time frame. I place my order to liquidate just below that spot in a long position or just above that spot in a short position. I place my orders just above or just below because I don't care about squeezing the last tic out of the trade. I have found over the years that trying to do that just isn't worth it.

One other factor you need to take into consideration is your risk-to-reward ratio. The risk-to-reward ratio is the dollar value of how much risk you have to take relative to the profit potential. Ideally, your risk-to-reward ratio should be at least 3:1, which means you are only risking one dollar for every three dollars of profit potential. If your edge and the way you scale out of your trades give you a 3:1 risk-to-reward ratio, your winning trade percentage can be less than 50 percent and you will still make money consistently.

A 3:1 risk-to-reward ratio is ideal. However, for the purposes of this exercise, it doesn't matter what it is, nor does it matter how effectively you scale out, as long as you do it. Do the best you can to pay yourself at reasonable profit levels when the market makes the money available. Every portion of a trade that you take off as a winner will contribute to your belief that you are a consistent winner. All the numbers will eventually come into better alignment as your belief in your ability to be consistent becomes stronger.

Trading in Sample Sizes. The typical trader practically lives or dies (emotionally) on the results of the most recent trade. If it was a winner, he'll gladly go to the next trade; if it wasn't, he'll start questioning the viability of his edge. To find out what variables work, how well they work, and what doesn't work, we need a systematic approach, one that doesn't take any random variables into consideration. This means that we have to expand our definition of success or failure from the limited trade-by-trade perspective of the typical trader to a sample size of 20 trades or more.

Any edge you decide on will be based on some limited number of market variables or relationships between those variables that measure the market's potential to move either up or down. From the market's perspective, each trader who has the potential to put on or take off a trade can act as a force on price movement and is, therefore, a market variable. No edge or technical system can take into consideration every trader and his reasons for putting on or taking off a trade. As a result, any set of market variables that defines an edge is like a snapshot of something very fluid, capturing only a limited portion of all the possibilities.

When you apply any set of variables to the market, they may work very well over an extended period of time, but after a while you may find that their effectiveness diminishes. That's because the underlying dynamics of the interaction between all the participants (the market) is changing. New traders come into the market with their own unique ideas of what is high and what is low, and other traders leave. Little by little, these changes affect the underlying dynamics of how the market moves. No snapshot (rigid set of variables) can take these subtle changes into consideration.

You can compensate for these subtle changes in the underlying dynamics of market movement and still maintain a consistent approach by trading in sample sizes. Your sample size has to be large enough to give your variables a fair and adequate test, but at the same time small enough so that if their effectiveness diminishes, you can detect it before you lose an inordinate amount of money. I have found that a sample size of at least 20 trades fulfills both of these requirements.

Testing. Once you decide on a set of variables that conform to these specifications, you need to test them to see how well they work. If you have the appropriate software to do this, you are probably already familiar with the procedures. If you don't have testing software, you can either forward test your variables or hire a testing service to do it for you. If you need a recommendation for a testing service, contact me at *markdouglas.com* or *tradinginthezone.com* for a referral. In any case, keep in mind that the object of the exercise is to use trading as a vehicle to learn how to think objectively (in the market's perspective), as if you were a casino operator. Right now, the bottom-line performance of your system isn't very important, but it is important that you have a good idea of what you can expect in the way of a win-to-loss ratio (the number of winning trades relative to the number of losing trades for your sample size).

Accepting the Risk. A requirement of this exercise is that you know in advance exactly what your risk is on each trade in your 20-trade sample size. As you now know, knowing the risk and accepting the risk are two different things. I want you to be as comfortable as possible with the dollar value of the risk you are taking in this exercise. Becuse the exercise requires that you use a 20-trade sample size, the potential risk is that you will lose on all 20 trades. This is obviously the worst-case scenario. It is as likely an occurrence as that you will win on all 20 trades, which means it isn't very likely. Nevertheless, it is a possibility. Therefore, you should set up the exercise in such a way that you can accept the risk (in dollar value) of losing on all 20 trades.

For example, if you're trading S&P futures, your edge might require that you risk three full points per contract to find out if the trade is going to work. Since the exercise requires that you trade a minimum of three contracts per trade, the total dollar value of the risk per trade is $2,250, if you use big contracts. The accumulated dollar value of risk if you lose on all 20 trades is $45,000. You may not be comfortable risking $45,000 on this exercise.

If you're not comfortable, you can reduce the dollar value of the risk by trading S&P mini contracts (E-Mini). They are one-fifth the value of the big contracts, so the total dollar value of the risk per trade goes down to $450 and the accumulated risk for all 20 trades is $9,000. You can do the same thing if you are trading stocks: Just keep on reducing the number of shares per trade until you get to a point where you are comfortable with the total accumulated risk for all 20 trades.

What I don't want you to do is change your established risk parameters to satisfy your comfort levels. If, based on your research, you have determined that a three-point risk in the S&Ps is the optimum distance you must let the market trade against your edge to tell you it isn't worth staying in the position, then leave it at three points. Change this variable only if it is warranted from a technical analysis perspective.

If you've done everything possible to reduce your position size and find that you still aren't comfortable with the accumulated dollar value of losing on all 20 trades, then I suggest you do the exercise with a simulated brokerage service. With a simulated brokerage service, everything about the process of putting on and taking off trades, including fills and brokerage statements, is exactly the same as with an actual brokerage firm, except that the trades are not actually entered into the market. As a result, you don't actually have any money at risk. A simulated brokerage service is an excellent tool to practice with in real time, under real market conditions; it is also an excellent tool for forward testing a trading system. There may be others, but the only service of this nature that I know of is *Auditrack.com*.

Doing the Exercise. When you have a set of variables that conforms to the specifications described, you know exactly what each trade is going to cost to find out if it's going to work, you have a plan for taking profits, and you know what you can expect as a win-loss ratio for your sample size, then you are ready to begin the exercise.

The rules are simple: Trade your system exactly as you have designed it. This means you have to commit yourself to trading at least the next 20 occurrences of your edge—not just the next trade or the next couple of trades, but all 20, no matter what. You cannot deviate, use or be influenced by any other extraneous factors, or change the variables that define your edge until you have completed a full sample size.

By setting up the exercise with rigid variables that define your edge, relatively fixed odds, and a commitment to take every trade in your sample size, you have created a trading regime that duplicates how a casino operates. Why do casinos make consistent money on an event that has a random outcome? Because they know that over a series of events, the odds are in their favor. They also know that to realize the benefits of the favorable odds, they have to participate in every event. They can't engage in a process of picking and choosing which hand of blackjack, spin of the roulette wheel, or roll of the dice they are going to participate in, by trying to predict in advance the outcome of each of these individual events.

If you believe in the five fundamental truths and you believe that trading is just a probability game, not much different from pulling the handle of a slot machine, then you'll find that this exercise will be effortless—effortless because your desire to follow through with your commitment to take every trade in your sample size and your belief in the probabilistic nature of trading will be in complete harmony. As a result, there will be no fear, resistance, or distracting thoughts. What could stop you from doing exactly what you need to do, when you need to do it, without reservation or hesitation? Nothing!

On the other hand, if it hasn't already occurred to you, this exercise is going to create a head-on collision between your desire to think objectively in probabilities and all the forces inside you that are in conflict with this desire. The amount of difficulty you have in doing this exercise will be in direct proportion to the degree to which these conflicts exist. To one degree or another, you will experience the exact opposite of what I described in the previous paragraph. Don't be surprised if you find your first couple of attempts at doing this exercise virtually impossible.

How should you handle these conflicts? Monitor yourself and use the technique of self-discipline to refocus on your objective. Write down the five fundamental truths and the seven principles of consistency, and keep them in front of you at all times when you are trading. Repeat them to yourself frequently, with conviction. Every time you notice that you are thinking, saying, or doing something that is inconsistent with these truths or principles, acknowledge the conflict. Don't try to deny the existence of conflicting forces. They are simply parts of your psyche that are (understandably) arguing for their versions of the truth.

When this happens, refocus on exactly what you are trying to accomplish. If your purpose is to think objectively, disrupt the association process (so you can stay in the "now moment opportunity flow"); step through your fears of being wrong, losing money, missing out, and leaving money on the table (so you can stop making errors and start trusting yourself), then you'll know exactly what you need to do. Follow the rules of your trading regime as best you can. Doing exactly what your rules call for while focused on the five fundamental truths will eventually resolve all your conflicts about the true nature of trading.

Every time you actually do something that confirms one of the five fundamental truths, you will be drawing energy out of the conflicting beliefs and adding energy to a belief in probabilities and in your ability to produce consistent results. Eventually, your new beliefs will become so powerful that it will take no conscious effort on your part to think and act in a way that is consistent with your objectives.

You will know for sure that thinking in probabilities is a functioning part of your identity when you will be able to go through one sample size of at least 20 or more trades without any difficulty, resistance, or conflicting thoughts distracting you from doing exactly what your mechanical system calls for. Then, and only then, will you be ready to move into the more advanced subjective or intuitive stages of trading.

A FINAL NOTE

Try not to prejudge how long it will take before you can get through at least one sample size of trades, following your plan without deviation, distracting thoughts, or hesitation to act. It will take as long as it takes. If you wanted to be a professional golfer, it wouldn't be unusual to dedicate yourself to hitting 10,000 or more golf balls until the precise combination of movements in your swing were so ingrained in your muscle memory that you no longer had to think about it consciously.

When you're out there hitting those golf balls, you aren't playing an actual game against someone or winning the big tournament. You do it because you believe that skill acquisition and practice will help you win. Learning to be a consistent winner as a trader isn't any different.

I wish you great prosperity, and would say "good luck," but you really won't need luck if you work at acquiring the appropriate skills.

ATTITUDE SURVEY

1. To make money as a trader you have to know what the market is going to do next.

   Agree   **Disagree**

2. Sometimes I find myself thinking that there must be a way to trade without having to take a loss.

   Agree   **Disagree**

3. Making money as a trader is primarily a function of analysis.

   Agree   **Disagree**

4. Losses are an unavoidable component of trading.

   Agree   **Disagree**

5. My risk is always defined before I enter a trade.

   Agree   **Disagree**

6. In my mind there is always a cost associated with finding out what the market may do next.

   Agree   **Disagree**

7. I wouldn't even bother putting on the next trade if I wasn't sure that it was going to be a winner.

   Agree   **Disagree**

8. The more a trader learns about the markets and how they behave, the easier it will be for him to execute his trades.

   Agree   **Disagree**

9. My methodology tells me exactly under what market conditions to either enter or exit a trade.

   Agree   **Disagree**

10. Even when I have a clear signal to reverse my position, I find it extremely difficult to do.

    Agree   **Disagree**

11. I have sustained periods of consistent success usually followed by some fairly drastic draw-downs in my equity.

    Agree   **Disagree**

12. When I first started trading I would describe my trading methodology as haphazard, meaning some success in between a lot of pain.

    Agree   **Disagree**

13. I often find myself feeling that the markets are against me personally.

    Agree   **Disagree**

14. As much as I might try to "let go," I find it very difficult to put past emotional wounds behind me.

    Agree   **Disagree**

15. I have a money management philosophy that is founded in the principle of always taking some money out of the market when the market makes it available.

    Agree   **Disagree**

16. A trader's job is to identify patterns in the markets' behavior that represent an opportunity and then to determine the risk of finding out if these patterns will play themselves out as they have in the past.

   Agree   **Disagree**

17. Sometimes I just can't help feeling that I am a victim of the market.

   Agree   **Disagree**

18. When I trade I usually try to stay focused in one time frame.

   Agree   **Disagree**

19. Trading successfully requires a degree of mental flexibility far beyond the scope of most people.

   Agree   **Disagree**

20. There are times when I can definitely feel the flow of the market; however, I often have difficulty acting on these feelings.

   Agree   **Disagree**

21. There are many times when I am in a profitable trade and I know the move is basically over, but I still won't take my profits.

   Agree   **Disagree**

22. No matter how much money I make in a trade, I am rarely ever satisfied and feel that I could have made more.

   Agree   **Disagree**

23. When I put on a trade, I feel I have a positive attitude. I anticipate all of the money I could make from the trade in a positive way.

    Agree   **Disagree**

24. The most important component in a trader's ability to accumulate money over time is having a belief in his own consistency.

    Agree   **Disagree**

25. If you were granted a wish to be able to instantaneously acquire one trading skill, what skill would you choose?

    _____

26. I often spend sleepless nights worrying about the market.

    Agree   **Disagree**

27. Do you ever feel compelled to make a trade because you are afraid that you might miss out?

    Yes   **No**

28. Although it doesn't happen very often, I really like my trades to be perfect. When I make a perfect call it feels so good that it makes up for all of the times that I don't.

    Agree   **Disagree**

29. Do you ever find yourself planning trades you never execute, and executing trades you never planned?

    Yes   **No**

30. In a few sentences explain why most traders either don't make money or aren't able to keep what they make.

_____

_____

_____

_____

INDEX